Santa Monica Airport
Jr. Aviator Logbook

Established in 1917
Serving the community for 100 years

Research and history by Linda-Marie Koerner
DC-3 Logo by Kate Cochrane

Welcome to the Santa Monica Airport!

The Santa Monica Airport was established as an informal landing strip in 1917 and is now celebrating its 100th year of serving the community.

Jr. Aviators: With this book you can log your visits to the Santa Monica Airport and learn what it takes to someday become a pilot. This book has hundreds of resources you can use to learn about aviation. Bring it with you each time you visit the Santa Monica Airport to observe planes and learn from pilots.

Parents: The second half of this book is designed for you with stories, historical facts and resources you might enjoy.

This book belongs to this Jr. Aviator:

Name: _________________

Age/Grade: _________________

Date: _________________

City, State: _________________

If lost, please return to this parent:

Name: _________________

Phone: _________________

Table of Contents

Part 1

Kids: Record your airport visits

Kids, use this section to record your visits to the Santa Monica Airport observation deck. Be sure to observe all the planes that land and take off. Then enter their information into these pages.

Run out of space? Not a problem!

Visit **SantaMonicaAirport.com** to get another copy of this book.

Santa Monica Airport Visit #1!

Today's date: _

Plane colors: _

Today, I saw:

☐ Propeller planes ☐ Jets

☐ Helicopters ☐ Parked planes

☐ Planes taxiing ☐ Police car

☐ Airport fire truck ☐ Fuel truck

☐ The Windsock ☐ A blimp!

☐ Air Traffic Control Tower

How many planes were there?

☐ Lots and lots! ☐ Lots ☐ Some ☐ Hardly any

The weather was:

☐ Sunny ☐ Cloudy

☐ Windy ☐ Cold

☐ Rainy ☐ Hot

I visited in the:

☐ Morning ☐ Lunchtime

☐ Afternoon ☐ Sunset

☐ Evening

Other fun airport places I went today:

☐ Park ☐ Spitfire Grill ☐ Museum ☐ DC-3 Monument

Insert plane tail numbers and other notes here:

Santa Monica Airport Visit #2!

Today's date: _ _ _ _ _ _ _ _ _ _ _ _ _ _ _ _ _

Plane colors: _ _ _ _ _ _ _ _ _ _ _ _ _ _ _ _ _

Today, I saw:

☐ Propeller planes   ☐ Jets

☐ Helicopters   ☐ Parked planes

☐ Planes taxiing   ☐ Police car

☐ Airport fire truck   ☐ Fuel truck

☐ The Windsock   ☐ A blimp!

☐ Air Traffic Control Tower

How many planes were there?

☐ Lots and lots!   ☐ Lots   ☐ Some   ☐ Hardly any

The weather was:

☐ Sunny   ☐ Cloudy

☐ Windy   ☐ Cold

☐ Rainy   ☐ Hot

I visited in the:

☐ Morning   ☐ Lunchtime

☐ Afternoon   ☐ Sunset

☐ Evening

Other fun airport places I went today:

☐ Park   ☐ Spitfire Grill   ☐ Museum   ☐ DC-3 Monument

Insert plane tail numbers and other notes here:

Santa Monica Airport Visit #3!

Today's date: _ _ _ _ _ _ _ _ _ _ _ _ _ _ _ _ _ _ _

Plane colors: _ _ _ _ _ _ _ _ _ _ _ _ _ _ _ _ _ _ _

Today, I saw:

☐ Propeller planes ☐ Jets

☐ Helicopters ☐ Parked planes

☐ Planes taxiing ☐ Police car

☐ Airport fire truck ☐ Fuel truck

☐ The Windsock ☐ A blimp!

☐ Air Traffic Control Tower

How many planes were there?

☐ Lots and lots!   ☐ Lots   ☐ Some   ☐ Hardly any

The weather was:

☐ Sunny ☐ Cloudy

☐ Windy ☐ Cold

☐ Rainy ☐ Hot

I visited in the:

☐ Morning ☐ Lunchtime

☐ Afternoon ☐ Sunset

☐ Evening

Other fun airport places I went today:

☐ Park   ☐ Spitfire Grill   ☐ Museum   ☐ DC-3 Monument

Insert plane tail numbers and other notes here:

Santa Monica Airport Visit #4!

Today's date: _ _ _ _ _ _ _ _ _ _ _ _ _ _ _ _ _

Plane colors: _ _ _ _ _ _ _ _ _ _ _ _ _ _ _ _ _

Today, I saw:

☐ Propeller planes   ☐ Jets

☐ Helicopters   ☐ Parked planes

☐ Planes taxiing   ☐ Police car

☐ Airport fire truck   ☐ Fuel truck

☐ The Windsock   ☐ A blimp!

☐ Air Traffic Control Tower

How many planes were there?

☐ Lots and lots!   ☐ Lots   ☐ Some   ☐ Hardly any

The weather was:

☐ Sunny   ☐ Cloudy

☐ Windy   ☐ Cold

☐ Rainy   ☐ Hot

I visited in the:

☐ Morning   ☐ Lunchtime

☐ Afternoon   ☐ Sunset

☐ Evening

Other fun airport places I went today:

☐ Park   ☐ Spitfire Grill   ☐ Museum   ☐ DC-3 Monument

Insert plane tail numbers and other notes here:

Santa Monica Airport Visit #5!

Today's date: _____________________

Plane colors: _____________________

Today, I saw:

☐ Propeller planes   ☐ Jets

☐ Helicopters   ☐ Parked planes

☐ Planes taxiing   ☐ Police car

☐ Airport fire truck   ☐ Fuel truck

☐ The Windsock   ☐ A blimp!

☐ Air Traffic Control Tower

How many planes were there?

☐ Lots and lots!   ☐ Lots   ☐ Some   ☐ Hardly any

The weather was:

☐ Sunny   ☐ Cloudy

☐ Windy   ☐ Cold

☐ Rainy   ☐ Hot

I visited in the:

☐ Morning   ☐ Lunchtime

☐ Afternoon   ☐ Sunset

☐ Evening

Other fun airport places I went today:

☐ Park   ☐ Spitfire Grill   ☐ Museum   ☐ DC-3 Monument

Insert plane tail numbers and other notes here:

Santa Monica Airport Visit #6!

Today's date: _ _ _ _ _ _ _ _ _ _ _ _ _ _ _ _ _ _ _

Plane colors: _ _ _ _ _ _ _ _ _ _ _ _ _ _ _ _ _ _ _

Today, I saw:

☐ Propeller planes ☐ Jets

☐ Helicopters ☐ Parked planes

☐ Planes taxiing ☐ Police car

☐ Airport fire truck ☐ Fuel truck

☐ The Windsock ☐ A blimp!

☐ Air Traffic Control Tower

How many planes were there?

☐ Lots and lots! ☐ Lots ☐ Some ☐ Hardly any

The weather was:

☐ Sunny ☐ Cloudy

☐ Windy ☐ Cold

☐ Rainy ☐ Hot

I visited in the:

☐ Morning ☐ Lunchtime

☐ Afternoon ☐ Sunset

☐ Evening

Other fun airport places I went today:

☐ Park ☐ Spitfire Grill ☐ Museum ☐ DC-3 Monument

Insert plane tail numbers and other notes here:

Santa Monica Airport Visit #7!

Today's date: _ _ _ _ _ _ _ _ _ _ _ _ _ _ _ _ _ _ _

Plane colors: _ _ _ _ _ _ _ _ _ _ _ _ _ _ _ _ _ _ _

Today, I saw:

☐ Propeller planes   ☐ Jets

☐ Helicopters   ☐ Parked planes

☐ Planes taxiing   ☐ Police car

☐ Airport fire truck   ☐ Fuel truck

☐ The Windsock   ☐ A blimp!

☐ Air Traffic Control Tower

How many planes were there?

☐ Lots and lots!   ☐ Lots   ☐ Some   ☐ Hardly any

The weather was:

☐ Sunny   ☐ Cloudy

☐ Windy   ☐ Cold

☐ Rainy   ☐ Hot

I visited in the:

☐ Morning   ☐ Lunchtime

☐ Afternoon   ☐ Sunset

☐ Evening

Other fun airport places I went today:

☐ Park   ☐ Spitfire Grill   ☐ Museum   ☐ DC-3 Monument

Insert plane tail numbers and other notes here:

Santa Monica Airport Visit #8!

Today's date: _ _ _ _ _ _ _ _ _ _ _ _ _ _ _ _ _

Plane colors: _ _ _ _ _ _ _ _ _ _ _ _ _ _ _ _ _

Today, I saw:

☐ Propeller planes ☐ Jets

☐ Helicopters ☐ Parked planes

☐ Planes taxiing ☐ Police car

☐ Airport fire truck ☐ Fuel truck

☐ The Windsock ☐ A blimp!

☐ Air Traffic Control Tower

How many planes were there?

☐ Lots and lots! ☐ Lots ☐ Some ☐ Hardly any

The weather was:

☐ Sunny ☐ Cloudy

☐ Windy ☐ Cold

☐ Rainy ☐ Hot

I visited in the:

☐ Morning ☐ Lunchtime

☐ Afternoon ☐ Sunset

☐ Evening

Other fun airport places I went today:

☐ Park ☐ Spitfire Grill ☐ Museum ☐ DC-3 Monument

Insert plane tail numbers and other notes here:

Part 2

Learn how planes fly

Kids, this area is designed for you to learn how airplanes fly! These pages will guide you through many of the parts of an airplane and the airport. Some of these pages are interactive, you can fill them out while you are at the airport. Be sure to bring pen or pencil so you can mark down what you see!

I spotted airplanes and saw these parts of airplanes

I know the parts of the plane and what they do!

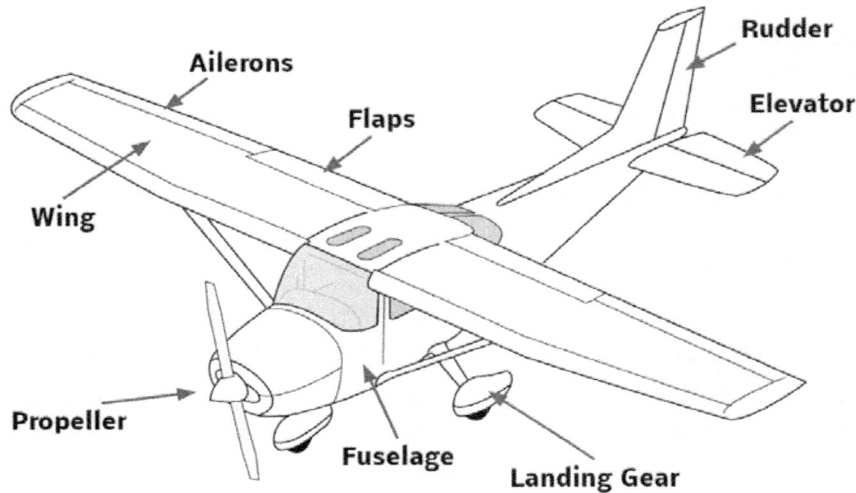

Check the box if you saw each part of the plane:

☐ **Propeller** – A propeller "lifts" an airplane forward. Think of a propeller as a spinning wing. Like a wing, it produces lift, but in a forward direction.

☐ **Engine** – The engine creates power to turn the propeller. Sometimes engines are at the front of the plane, sometimes they are on the back, and sometimes there are two (one on each wing).

☐ **Fuselage** – The long part of the plane. This is where the pilot sits.

☐ **Wing** – The wing creates the lift that makes the plane fly. Sometimes the wings are on top of the plane and sometimes they are on the bottom of the plane.

□ **Landing gear** – The landing gear includes the wheels with the tires that let the plane land and drive around on the ground. Sometimes they fold up inside the plane. This is called a retractable landing gear.

□ **Flaps** – The flaps are small moving parts at the back of the wing that let the pilot change the shape of the wing. They help the wing create more lift so that the plane can fly slower.

□ **Ailerons** – The ailerons help the plane bank and roll to the right and left. See the next page to learn how a "roll" works.

□ **Elevator** – The elevator lets the plane climb and descend by changing the pitch of the plane.

□ **Rudder** – The rudder moves side to side and makes the plane turn to the right or left. Usually the rudder is used with the ailerons. When you use both together, it is called a coordinated turn.

What are Flight Control Surfaces?

The pilot uses the controls in the cockpit to make different parts of the airplane move. The airplane flies differently in the sky when these parts move.

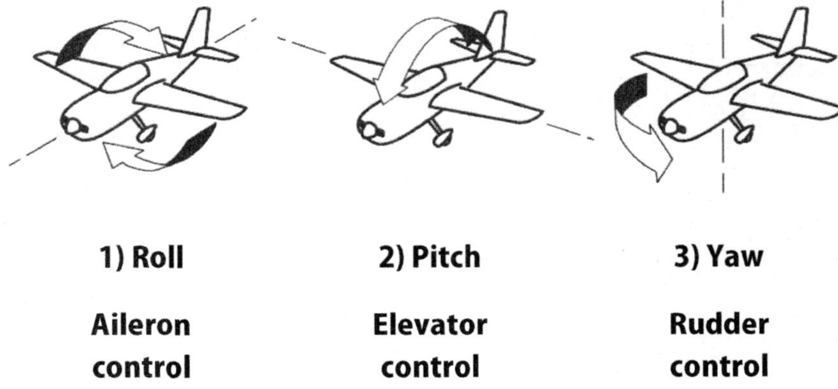

1. When the ailerons on the wings move, one goes up and the other goes down. This makes the plane roll, or bank.
2. When the elevator on the tail moves up and down, the nose of the plane pitches up and down.
3. When the vertical part of the tail, the rudder, moves side to side, the plane makes a flat, directional turn, right and left.

The pilot uses all the different controls to smoothly operate the airplane.

How does the wing work?

The shape of the wing changes the pressure of the air around it, producing more pressure under the wing and less pressure on top of it. This creates lift and helps the plane go up in the air.

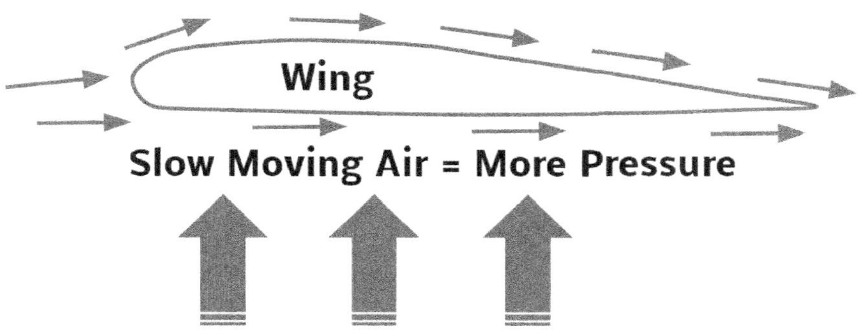

The Four Forces of Flight

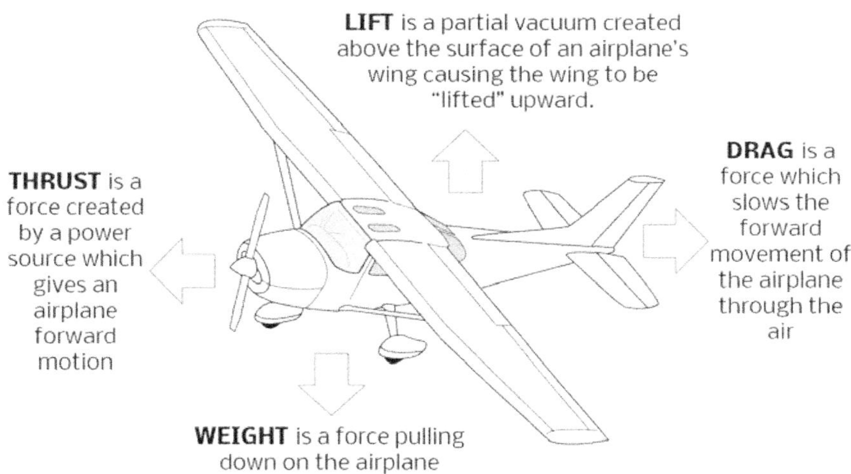

Runway numbers: What do they mean?

You hear controllers and pilots saying runway numbers like "Runway two one" or "Runway three." Runways are numbered by the direction they point. You figure out using a compass.

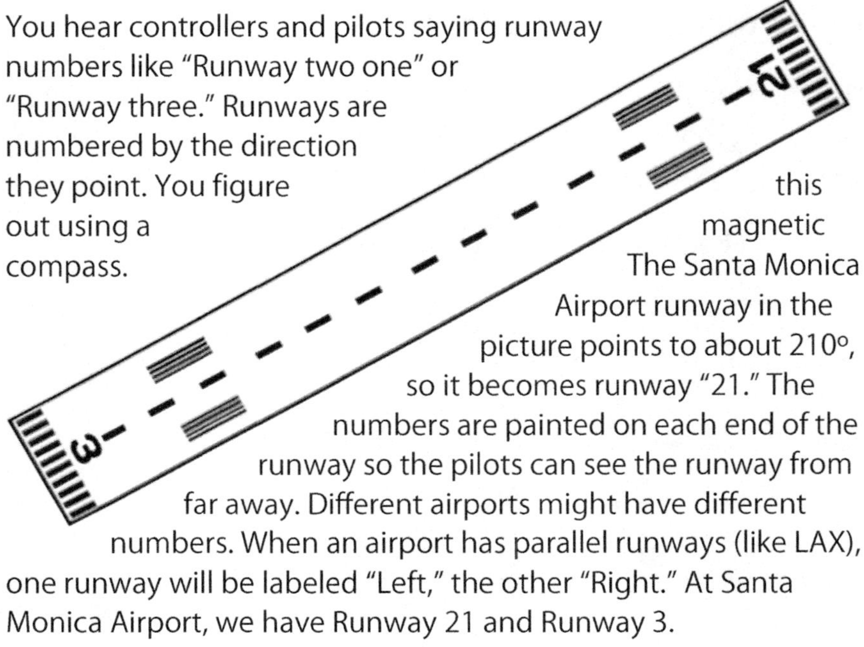

this magnetic The Santa Monica Airport runway in the picture points to about 210º, so it becomes runway "21." The numbers are painted on each end of the runway so the pilots can see the runway from far away. Different airports might have different numbers. When an airport has parallel runways (like LAX), one runway will be labeled "Left," the other "Right." At Santa Monica Airport, we have Runway 21 and Runway 3.

But why do runways point a certain direction?

Runways are laid down on the ground into the direction of the most wind!

Aircraft take off best when they fly into the direction of the wind. The more wind over their wings the shorter runway they need to take off.

Have you ever noticed a bunch of birds sitting together on a wire? They usually face the same way. This isn't because they can't think for themselves. It's because they are all facing into the wind, so when they hop off the wire into the wind, they will take off more easily.

So, when people make airports, they angle the runways into the direction the wind usually blows.

Does the wind always blow the same direction?

In Santa Monica, the enormous Pacific Ocean is much cooler than the land we walk around on. So as the day goes on, the sun heats up the ground and the air around us gets warmer and rises up into the sky! When that happens, the air over the ocean moves toward the space where the warm air used to be. Then, the ocean air blows onto the beach, onto the land and right down the runway of the airport!

The direction of this wind from off the ocean is usually 210 degrees (measured from the magnetic north pole).

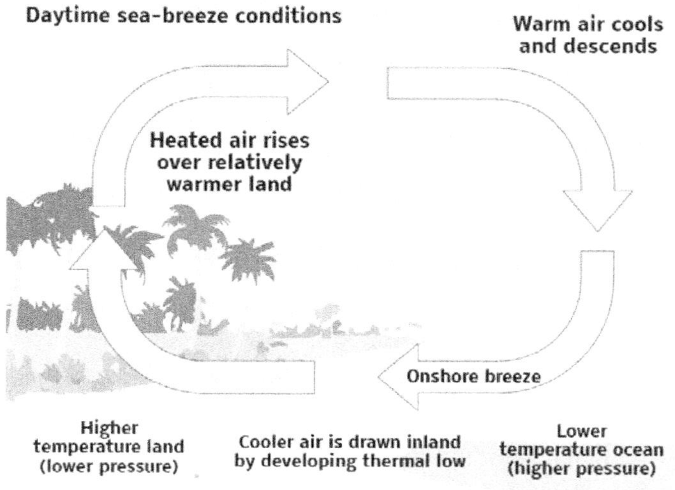

If you pay attention, you can start to notice when this ocean breeze starts. Sometimes it is at about 1 in the afternoon.

This whole process reverses at night, but that wind is not as strong.

There is other weather at Santa Monica Airport, but this breeze off the ocean happens often enough that the runway was set up to take maximum advantage of it.

Sometimes when there are strong winds coming off the desert, the aircraft at Santa Monica Airport and LAX take off in the other direction (away from the ocean). In that case, the aircraft takeoff in an eastern direction on the same runway, but they call it by its other number, runway 3.

The Air Traffic Control Tower

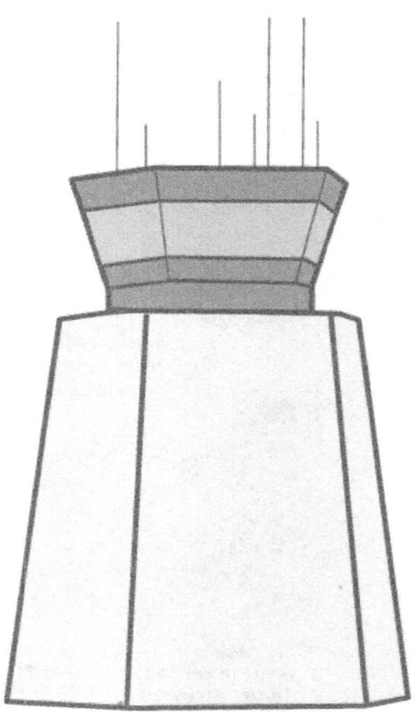

The Santa Monica Air Traffic Control Tower is 75 feet tall and has 2 to 3 highly trained professionals known as air traffic controllers working inside. They talk to planes and direct them on the ground and in the air. When you are at the Airport Observation Deck, you can listen to the loud speakers and hear the controllers talking to the pilots.

The Santa Monica Airport Beacon

The airport beacon is 50 feet tall. It has a green and white light that spins around and can be seen for miles. The light is turned on from dusk until dawn. Generally, it is turned on days when you can't see for three miles on the ground or 1,000 feet up into the sky. Have you ever seen the beacon when it is lit? Look for it!

I have seen the beacon lit up!

☐ On a gray and foggy day

☐ On a rainy, stormy day

☐ In the evening

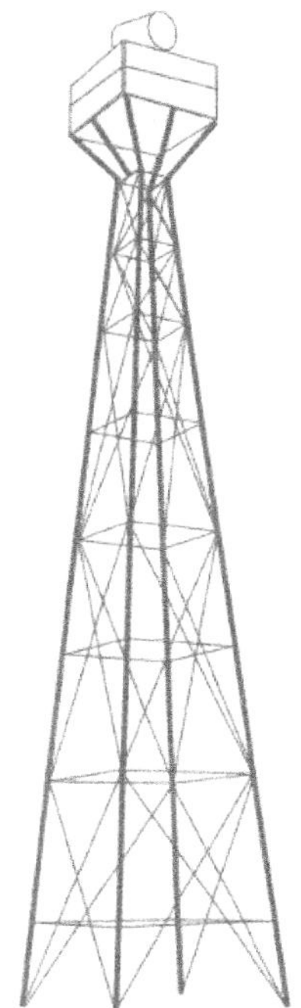

The Rotating Beacon Tower represents one of the earliest navigational tools used in night flying. In the early air mail days of 1923, the Post Office worked to complete a transcontinental airway of beacons on towers spaced 15 to 25 miles apart, each with enough brightness to be seen for 40 miles in clear weather. By June 1927, about 4,121 miles of airways had lights. By 1933, about 18,000 miles of airway and 1,500 beacons were in place. The tower at Santa Monica Airport was part of the San Diego – Los Angeles national airway system and was moved from its original installation in Downey in 1952. (SOURCE: SantaMonicaLandmarks.com)

How to talk like a pilot!

Ever heard pilots talk on the radio and wonder what they're saying? You can hear them in the speaker at the Santa Monica Airport observation deck. It sounds confusing, but it's really not.

We can show you how to understand what pilots say.

Who are you?

Well, you are an aircraft. You have a number, painted on your tail, and you identify yourself on the radio as that number. You could be Cessna N172EP, or Helicopter N63L or Lightsport N126WK. Instead of answering to your name, you answer to this number when you talk on the radio.

Saying letters uses a fun code (be sure to see the "aviation alphabet" on page 25). Since some letters sound like other letters, it's safer to say a whole word to represent each letter so we can differentiate between them. The letter "N" becomes "November," "L" is "Lima," "E" is "Echo," "B" is "Bravo," and so on.

Why do some planes have shorter call signs?

Let's assume you are flying Lightsport November One Two Six Whiskey Kilo (N126WK). That takes a long time to say every letter, every time, so the tower will shorten your call sign to the last three digits once they are familiar with who you are (and what you want to do).

However, pilots are only allowed to abbreviate their own call sign if the air traffic controller shortens it when they talk to you. You are "Lightsport 126WK" until an air traffic controller calls you "Lightsport 6WK."

What do I say on the radio?

This depends on what you want to do.

Let's say you want to taxi to the runway. Say this:

"Santa Monica Ground, Lightsport One Two Six Whiskey Kilo is at Santa Monica Flyers, request taxi southeast runup."

> **Runup:** A runup is the series of last-minute checks performed by pilots on an aircraft prior to take-off. Usually it is near the end of a runway. This ensures everything is running smoothly before takeoff.

In this case, the tower may grant you permission to taxi:

"Lightsport One Two Six Whiskey Kilo, Santa Monica Ground, taxi to the southeast runup."

Then you would reply:

"Taxi to the southeast runup, Lightsport One Two Six Whiskey Kilo."

Notice how you repeated their directions and then repeated your name at the end? This is because there may be many pilots talking on the radio. It's important to let the air traffic controllers know you heard them, what you understood and who you are. This makes sure there are no mistakes.

If you want to take off, you have to ask to approach the runway:

"Santa Monica Ground, Lightsport One Two Six Whiskey Kilo is at the southeast runup, request taxi runway 21."

They might respond with:

"Lightsport Six Whiskey Kilo Santa Monica Ground, taxi runway 21."

Notice how they shortened your call sign on that last transmission?

To take off, you might say something like this:

"Santa Monica Tower, Lightsport Six Whiskey Kilo is holding short runway 21, request right turn at the shoreline."

"Right turn at the shoreline" is what you say when you want to take off and turn right at the Santa Monica beach. This is a very common flight pattern at Santa Monica Airport.

The tower then might approve you for takeoff and say this:

"Lightsport Six Whiskey Kilo, Cleared for takeoff runway 21, right turn at the shoreline."

There's more to taking off, but that's a good start.

Let's say you are flying in from the Malibu area and want to land.

You might ask the tower this question:

"Santa Monica Tower, Lightsport One Two Six Whiskey Kilo is at position at 1,500 feet, inbound for landing."

The tower might respond with:

"Lightsport One Two Six Whiskey Kilo, Santa Monica Tower, make right traffic runway 21."

"Right Traffic, Runway 21" means you get to enter the traffic pattern near Santa Monica Airport.

You would need to confirm you heard them and you repeat back to them the instructions they gave you. This is called a "read back."

"Make right traffic runway 21, Lightsport One Two Six Whiskey Kilo."

When the tower is ready for you to land, they would say something like this. You need to hear the controller say the words "cleared to land" before you can land:

"Lightsport Six Whiskey Kilo, runway 21, cleared to land.

This is just the beginning of how to talk to the tower, but now you have an idea how the communication works.

At the Santa Monica Airport Observation Deck you can hear the controllers and pilots over the speaker. Listen for these phrases. Check off each box as you hear these phrases:

☐ **"Line up and wait."** An airplane has just landed, and the airport is busy. The tower has you taxi onto the runway and wait. As soon as the airplane who just landed is clear of the runway, the tower will have you take off.

What does it mean when a plane taxis? When a plane drives on the ground (like a car), it's called taxiing. This happens before takeoff, after a landing and anytime the plane is moving around on the ground.

☐ "Make short approach, cleared to land runway 21, Lightsport Six Whiskey Kilo."

☐ "Inbound for Landing using Runway two one." You are 6 miles away and will want to land on Runway two one.

☐ 'Roger, number two, cleared to land runway 21 Lightsport Six Whiskey Kilo.'

☐ '"Lightsport Six Whiskey Kilo, contact ground 121.9, good day."

☐ "Lightsport Six Whiskey Kilo, cleared for takeoff, Runway 21." You are cleared to take off on Runway 21.

You don't have to be at the airport to listen to the airport! You can listen to almost any airport in the country by visiting **LiveATC.net** on your phone or computer. You can hear super busy airports like LAX and less busy airports too!

Learn the Airfield Traffic Pattern

Traffic patterns are flown using all left-hand turns, or all right-hand turns. These are called "left traffic" or "right traffic" patterns.

They are usually left-hand turns because most airplanes are piloted from the left seat (or the pilot-in-command sits in the left seat), and the pilot has a better view of the runway (and other planes) out the left window.

When a pilot wants to practice takeoffs and landings, he or she will often fly around the pattern to practice.

To do this, they fly in a "left traffic pattern."

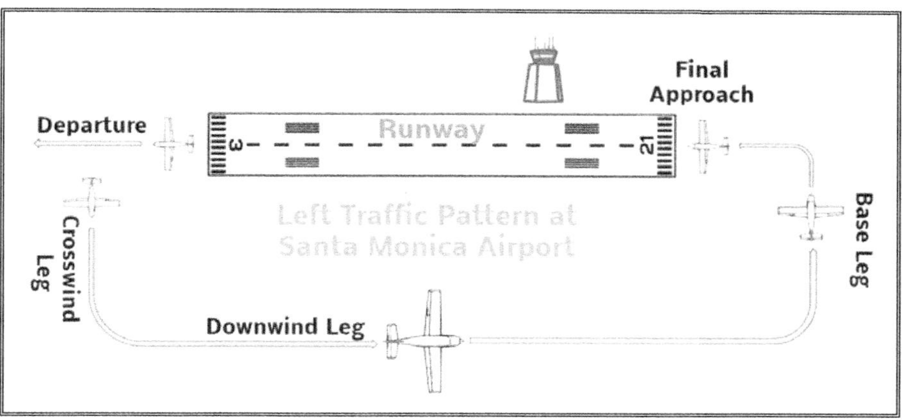

Each of these arrows has a name (check off each name when you see a plane flying on that leg):

☐ **Departure leg:** This is the climbing flight path using the runway, it begins at take off and continue at least 1/2 mile past the runway's departure end.

☐ **Crosswind leg:** A short climbing flight path at right angles to the departure end of the runway.

☐ **Downwind leg:** When a plane flies parallel to (but in the opposite direction) of the landing runway.

☐ **Base leg:** A short, descending flight path at right angles to the approach end of the landing runway.

☐ **Final approach:** A flight path in the direction of landing along the runway. The last section of the final approach is sometimes referred to as short final.

> **Why do smaller planes at Santa Monica Airport go left and cross over the golf course?** It's because houses under the plane experience the most noise, so the smaller planes voluntarily fly over the golf course to keep the noise over the open space—rather than people's homes—for as long as possible.

How does a windsock work?

A windsock is a tube that resembles a giant sock. They are usually orange and white and placed close to the runway for pilots to see them. Windsocks are used as a basic guide to gauge wind direction and speed. Most windsocks can sense wind as gentle as 3 knots (3.5 mph) and are fully extended at about 15 knots (17 mph).

They are calibrated for each section of the windsock to change shape at a different wind speed. See below for examples of the wind sock shapes.

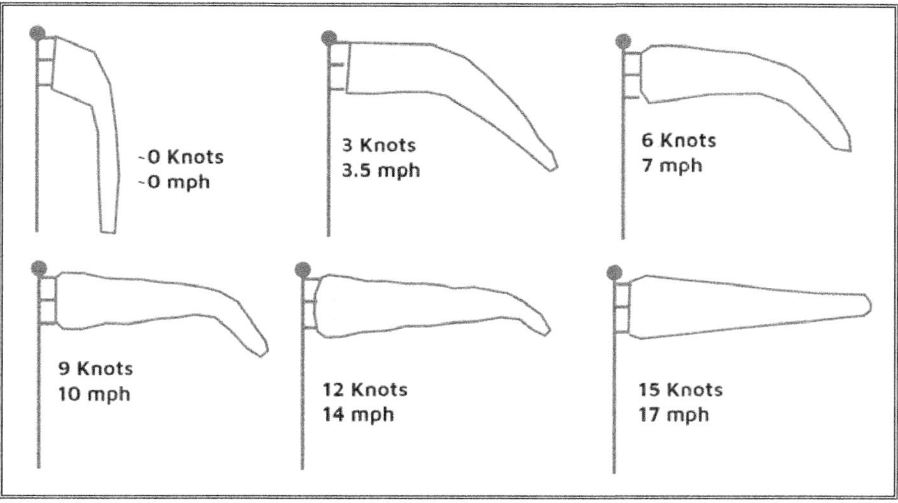

Windsocks are usually lit at night so pilots can see them. Sometimes there's a small light inside the windsock so it glows orange for pilots to easily be able to see its shape with a quick glance. Windsocks also spin around on the stick that holds them up. This shows you the direction the wind is blowing. The big, open part catches the wind. The skinny part points in the direction the wind is blowing.

Aviation Alphabet

Air Traffic Controllers and pilots use these words all the time. All aircraft have letters and numbers written on their tails. This is the aircraft's "name." The taxiways on the ground have letters too! So, the first taxiway is "alpha," the next is "bravo" and so on. Learn these letters and you can understand when the pilots and controllers talk on the radio!

Letter	Say This	Letter	Say This
A	Alpha	N	November
B	Bravo	O	Oscar
C	Charlie	P	Papa
D	Delta	Q	Quebec
E	Echo	R	Romeo
F	Foxtrot	S	Sierra
G	Golf	T	Tango
H	Hotel	U	Uniform
I	India	V	Victor
J	Juliet	W	Whiskey
K	Kilo	X	X-ray or Xray
L	Lima	Y	Yankee
M	Mike	Z	Zulu

Spell your name using the airport alphabet

Use the code! You can have fun and learn how to say your name using this code!

I spell my first name like this: _______________________________

My first name using this code is:

First Letter: _______________________________

Second Letter: _______________________________

Third Letter: _______________________________

Fourth Letter: _______________________________

Fifth Letter: _______________________________

Sixth Letter: _______________________________

Seventh Letter: _______________________________

Eighth Letter: _______________________________

Ninth Letter: _______________________________

Now say your name. If your name has more letters, just keep going!

What is a General Aviation Airport?

Well first, a commercial/scheduled aviation airport is any version of flying for hire. This includes airline operations. Large airports like LAX could be considered commercial aviation airports since most of their operations are scheduled.

General Aviation (GA) is the term for all civil aviation operations other than airlines/scheduled air services. Santa Monica Airport mostly serves general aviation purposes. General aviation flights range from single engine Cessnas (the little planes) to business jet flights. The majority of the world's air traffic falls into the general aviation category, and most of the world's airports serve general aviation exclusively. The main difference between personal flights and commercial flights is that someone gets paid to conduct commercial flights. The pilot in command of a commercial flight must have a commercial pilot certificate. For all other general aviation flights, a private pilot certificate is sufficient to act as pilot in command.

General Aviation Services

Police, fire, emergency medical services and search and rescue are some of the essential services provided to the public by general aviation airports like Santa Monica Airport. Also, services like Angel Flight West (page 34), Pilots N Paws (page 35), and flight training (page 47) rely on smaller general aviation airports for their work.

Part 3

Airport Programs and Interviews

Parents, included in this section are some of the programs and non-profit charitable organizations here at the airport. The interviews that follow are perfect for you to read to your kids as you share the photos. These interviews may inspire your kids to learn more about the interesting people who work at and around the airport!

Put your kid in a real airplane at our next event

Parents: Bring your kids on the ultimate field trip to the Santa Monica Airport observation deck to sit inside a real airplane and take a photo with a pilot.

Each kid gets to spend several minutes learning how a real plane works from a real pilot. They get to touch the steering wheel (yoke) and watch as the ailerons and rudder changes shape.

Our events have inspired 3,000+ kids all over Southern California to learn how aviation works.

We host these events at the Santa Monica Airport Observation Deck. This deck serves tens of thousands of locals each year. It provides access to view small airplanes for the youngest of aviators (and is fun for the whole family).

Airport events are announced each month. The best way to hear about them is to join our newsletter on our website.

Visit SantaMonicaAirport.com to learn more

Birthday Parties for Kids at Santa Monica Airport

Parents: Bring your kids to the public Santa Monica Airport Observation Deck to host the ultimate birthday party experience (and watch planes land from the open air flight deck).

This airplane experience is unlike any other in the world. Our great weather and small planes create a family-friendly environment for your kids (and their best friends).

We can create the ultimate experience for your group (up to 65 people) and allow each kid to learn about aviation at the same time.

Here's what you get:

- Airport stickers for the kids
- Bench seating for up to 20 people
- Public restrooms
- Free parking
- Great views of the public deck
- A real airplane and pilot to teach the kids (optional)

Visit SantaMonicaAirport.com/Birthday to learn more

Kids, Join a Young Eagles Event and Learn about Flying

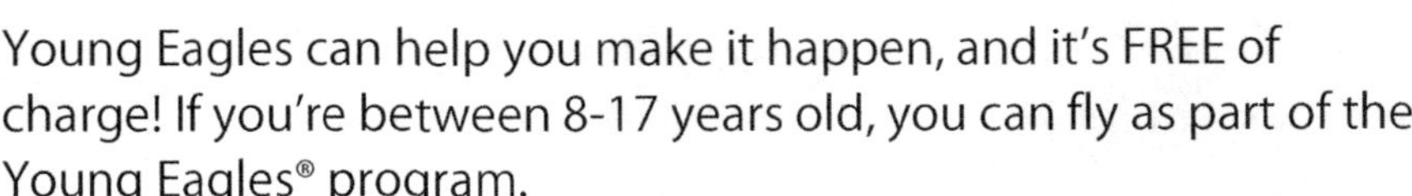

(For kids 8-17 years old)

Kids, do you think you might be interested in learning to fly? But maybe you've never been up in a private airplane, and you don't know anyone with an airplane. Does it all seem like it's just going to cost too much money?

Young Eagles can help you make it happen, and it's FREE of charge! If you're between 8-17 years old, you can fly as part of the Young Eagles® program.

Founded in 1992, the Young Eagles program has dedicated nearly 25 years to giving kids 8-17 their first free ride in an airplane.

It's the only program of its kind! Its only mission is to introduce and inspire kids in the world of aviation. Today, the Young Eagles program has flown over 2 million kids with the help of EAA's network of volunteer pilots and ground volunteers.

Learn more at SantaMonicaAirport.com/YoungEagles

Parents, Get a Discovery Flight over Los Angeles

The dream of flying is not just for kids!

Parents, you can dip your toe in the water and learn what it feels like to fly in a single-engine plane.

In a short discovery class, you can receive official classroom instruction from an FAA certified flight instructor on how to fly an airplane, learning the basics of aerodynamics, flight instruments and navigation systems.

Then, enjoy flying and experience the thrill of aviation in a real airplane. An instructor can take you over downtown LA or along the coast to Malibu (weather permitting for all three).

Fly the airplane hands-on, one control at a time, while enjoying the breathtaking view.

Learn more at SantaMonicaAirport.com/discovery

Angel Flight West

The ability to travel easily around the country is something most people take for granted. But for people in need, the financial, physical, and emotional burdens can make ordinary trips extraordinarily difficult.

That's when they turn to Angel Flight West. AFW's network of 1,400+ volunteer pilots fly their own planes, paying for all costs out of their own pockets, to make these critical journeys possible.

Headquartered at Santa Monica Airport, Angel Flight West manages the complex logistics of matching pilots with passengers, coordinating the flights, spreading the word among referral agencies, and continually recruiting new volunteers.

People who benefit from these flights—the passengers and their families, and any health care organizations involved—pay nothing at all, ever.

Local pilots love to fly. And they want to help! They are engineers, scientists, and teachers. Doctors, lawyers, and corporate executives. Young entrepreneurs and retired commercial pilots. They all have two things in common: They love to fly, and they want to help others.

Learn more at AngelFlightWest.org

Pilots N Paws Program

Pilots N Paws, a registered 501c3 charity, connects rescues, shelters, and foster animals with private pilots willing to provide free transport to a family willing to adopt the animal. Pilots N Paws has more than 5,000 pilot volunteers and more than 12,000 ground volunteers.

Most importantly, each year, the volunteers of Pilots N Paws save thousands of animals' lives. Those lives come in the form of any animal that can be transported using a plane. Dogs, cats, pigs, reptiles and rabbits are just a few species who have taken our flights.

With over 4 million no-longer-wanted pets euthanized each year, pet overpopulation is a big problem in the U.S. Pilots N Paws is helping to change that.

Learn more at PilotsNpaws.org

Interview with a Retired Airline Pilot

Retired United Airlines Pilot Harry Albaugh II describes his years of experience flying big planes around the world.

Harry Albaugh II with his wife, Chrisann at the Santa Monica Airport

What inspired you to want to fly?

My father was a military pilot, and I grew up around airplanes and pilots. When I was a kid in school, I remember the United States and Russia were in a race to the moon. President Kennedy challenged the people of the United States to "land a man on the moon and safely return him to earth before the end of the decade (1970)." He also said that "we (the American people) choose to do this not because it is easy, but because it is hard."

In 1961, when President Kennedy made his speech, I was 12 years old. With my father's guidance and President Kennedy's leadership, I was inspired to be a pilot, and maybe even an astronaut.

Did you learn on a little plane?

Yes. Small planes are great! My first flight lessons were in a Cessna 152 flying out of Santa Monica Airport (SMO). Many of the things I learned at SMO I used for the next 45 years of my flying career.

What was your first introductory flight like at SMO?

In 1970, I was 21 years old, in my 3rd year of college at USC, studying Aerospace Engineering. I had an Air Force ROTC scholarship that paid for all my tuition, books, and private pilot lessons at SMO.

I took my first introductory flight with an instructor from Clair Walter's Flight Academy at Santa Monica Airport. The instructor was very friendly and flew me around the SMO area in a Cessna 152.

I was a passenger as my instructor flew the airplane. I could see people playing on the beaches, the ocean to the west, big jet planes taking off from Los Angeles International Airport to the south, and mountains to the east.

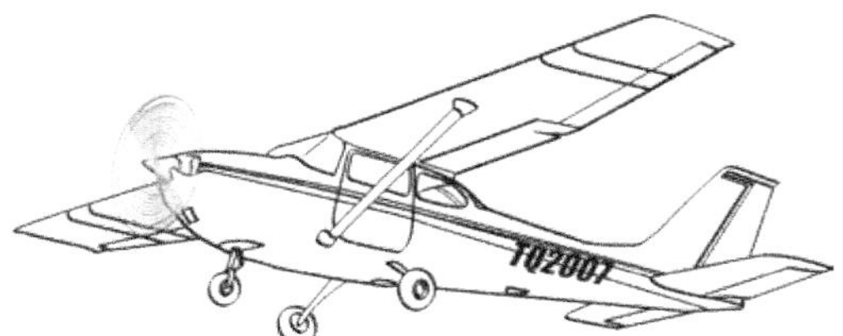

We returned to SMO and my instructor did a "touch-and-go" landing. That's where you fly to the runway, touch the wheels on the runway, and then take off again. After the "touch-and-go" landing, my instructor said "OK⋯It's now your turn to fly."

I was a little nervous, but I knew my instructor would talk to me and make sure that I would be okay. My instructor flew the airplane until we were at traffic-pattern altitude and flying parallel to the runway (downwind leg). He told me to take hold of the control wheel (the yoke) and fly the plane. I had to keep the wings level and maneuver the nose of the airplane up and down to maintain altitude. It was very different than driving a car, because I had to think about turning left and right as well as up and down.

At the correct time, the instructor told me to turn toward the runway, reduce the engine power, and descend all at the same time. It seemed like a lot to think about, but he helped me do it.

We maneuvered the airplane so that we were aligned with the runway and were descending, slowing down and putting out "flaps" down. The flaps are a part of the trailing edge of the wings. When you put them in the down position, they slow the airplane down and make it so the plane can fly at a slower speed for landing.

When we got to the runway, my instructor helped me reduce the engine power and pull back on the control wheel (yoke), all at the correct time. Pulling back on the control wheel makes the airplane stop descending and makes for a smooth touchdown on the runway. Reducing the throttle makes the engine slow down so you can land on the runway.

What a great introduction to flying. I was hooked. I knew that flying was something I wanted to do, and Santa Monica Airport (SMO) was a wonderful place to learn to fly.

What was it like learning to fly at SMO?

First, I attended "ground school" where I learned about the parts of the plane and how the wings make the plane fly. I also learned how the instruments in the cockpit work together and tell the pilot important things like how fast the plane is moving through the air, how fast the plane is going up (ascending) or down (descending), how the engine is working, and how much gas is onboard.

My first flight as a student was exciting.

I have fond memories of that first day of flying as a student at SMO. The things that I learned as a student at SMO served me well for the rest of my career as a military and civilian pilot.

Above: This is the runway at Santa Monica Airport. You can view it on your computer by visiting maps.google.com and clicking on the "earth" button at the bottom of the screen.

How many different planes have you learned to fly?

I got my private pilot license in 1970 at Santa Monica Municipal Airport (SMO) in a Cessna 150.

After graduating from college, I was commissioned as a 2nd Lieutenant in the U.S. Air Force and began Undergraduate Pilot Training (UPT) at Williams Air Force Base in Phoenix, Arizona.

My first trainer aircraft was a Cessna 172. My flight experience at SMO provided me with a solid footing to begin my Air Force pilot training.

The Cessna 172 was an initial trainer and was used to test a new student pilot's aptitude and ability to learn how to fly the "Air Force way." Some of the students did not have as good a foundation as I received at SMO and had a more difficult time than I did.

My next trainer was a T-37, centerline thrust, twin engine, fully acrobatic, subsonic "jet" trainer. The T-37 training course was about 6 months long. I learned about how to read charts and maps, and how to navigate in an airplane.

T-37 Air Force Trainer

After successfully passing the T-37 course, I began advanced training in the T-38 Talon. The T-38 is a sleek-looking, twin-engine, centerline-thrust, "supersonic" jet trainer. The T-38 can fly faster than the speed of sound and is fully acrobatic capable.

After Undergraduate Pilot Training, I spent 6 years in the Air Force and flew all over the world. I flew the KC-135, the EC-135, and the RC-135 (these airplanes are very similar to Air Force One at the Ronald Reagan Library).

Northrop T-38 Talon

After the Air Force, I flew for 35 years for United Airlines. I flew the Boeing-737, 757, 767, 747, and 777. I also flew the MacDonald Douglas DC-10 and the Airbus A-320.

I am now retired and can look back at my flying career and say that the training I received at SMO served me well.

What is your favorite part about flying?

I have lots of favorite parts about flying. I enjoy planning where I'm going to go (flight planning) because it gives me time to "preplay" what I am about to go do, what weather I can expect, and what sights I will probably be seeing.

My favorite part of every flight is takeoff and landing. When you are close to the ground, you can see how fast you are going. There are a lot of things going on, and it is a very busy time for the pilot.

Is it harder to fly a great big plane?

In big, modern jets we have today, there are a lot of computers and sophisticated electronics that reduce the work load on the pilot. But the truth is, if you shut all that stuff off, the basics of flight are the same as in the Cessna 150 that I flew at SMO at the start of my flying career.

Do you go many different places? Do you have a favorite?

As a professional pilot, I have flown all over the world. Mexico, Central America, South America, Europe, Australia, all over Asia are the many international places that I have flown to. Also all the major cities in the United States.

After visiting so many places all over world, my favorite place is still home.

Your father was a pilot in World War II. Where did he fly out of?

During the war, my father flew all over the world. He finished his wartime service in the China-India-Burma Theater. He completed 146 missions flying C-47's over the "rock pile" (the Himalayan Mountains) between India and Western China. As a modern-day jet pilot, I am amazed at what my father was able to do with the airplanes of that time. There's a good chance my father's C-47 aircraft was manufactured at Santa Monica Airport.

Retired Air Traffic Controller Interview

Pam Choi is a former air traffic controller who worked in the tower at SMO for 22 years and lives locally.

What does an air traffic controller do?

The air traffic controller helps the pilots get their planes to the runway to take off and land and fly through the air space safely.

How did you become an air traffic controller?

I saw a little ad in the newspaper: "Do you want to become an air traffic controller?" I applied! I applied to the Federal Aviation Administration for training, took their classes, was accepted and went to Tulsa, Oklahoma for more training. Once I passed, I was assigned to a tower, which was the Santa Monica tower, then I learned all about my tower. I didn't go to college to become an air traffic controller. I'm not a pilot. I got really good grades in high school and liked science and math. That helped.

What is the best part about being an air traffic controller?

The best part is being part of a team. The pilots, the air traffic controllers, the mechanics and everyone at the airport all work together to make air traffic safe. We depend on the pilots and the people we work with to make it all work. Also, it is wonderful to be able to help people when they need it. People in the air at Santa Monica are not alone in the sky.

Have you worked at many different airports? How are they different?

I have only worked as a controller at Santa Monica Airport, but I taught safety classes for 15 years travelling all over the country. There are basics that stay the same, but every place is different. It keeps it interesting—move to a new place, and it's all different.

Is there something about being an air traffic controller that you think people don't understand?

Some people think we're out on the airport waving flags around. We don't do that; we are in the tower. We don't just watch screens in the tower. We look outside! It is really important to look out the window at what is going on in the air.

What was/is your favorite aviation experience?

There are so many! One time I got to fly the Goodyear Blimp for about half an hour. I went up in the blimp and the pilots let me fly it for a short while. It was a blast!

If I want to be an air traffic controller, what should I do?

Study and get good grades. Do well in school. Read, learn about airplanes and flying. Math really helps, since some airplanes fly faster than others. You need to calculate which one will get to the airport first. Which plane will pass the other? It's called a "closure rate." Try to figure it out, think in three dimensions. Playing video and electronic games doesn't really help. It's more important to look outside and see what's going on. **Observe the outside world, focus, speak clearly, communicate well and work with others as a team. Also, go to the airport observation deck and listen to the tower and the aircraft, or listen to controllers all over the country on LiveATC.net!**

The First Non-Stop Flight Around The World

We interviewed record-breaking aviator Dick Rutan, who piloted the Voyager aircraft around the world non-stop with co-pilot Jeana Yeager.

What inspired you to get started in aviation?

I remember my very first aviation adventure vividly. I was six years old when my mother and I went to an old farm field for a true barnstorming ride. My mother was armed with a fist full of hard-earned dollar bills. We climbed into the old J5 Piper Cub and I begged my mother to let me stand so I could see out of the window. The little plane hopped and skipped down an old bumpy grass field, and after a struggle and a lot of engine noise, it was airborne. As I saw the earth beneath me, my view of how I wanted to see the world changed forever.

What is your favorite world record?

I have set and broken many records, but my favorite record will be the absolute record we set with the Voyager flight. It's a milestone record since it had never, ever been done before, and **we hold the record for being the first to fly nonstop, non-refueled around the world, in perpetuity.**

Tell us about the Voyager trip around the world.

In early December, 1986, Voyager was flown to Edwards Air Force Base in California. She was fueled for hours, and on December 14, 1986, Voyager took off on what would become The World's Longest Flight.

Voyager's flight was the first-ever, non-stop, unrefueled flight around the world. It took place between December 14 and December 23, 1986.

The Voyager was built in Mojave, California. It took five years to build and test the airplane before taking off on its record-setting flight.

There were two crew members on board, myself, and Jeana Yeager. My brother, Burt Rutan, who is a world-renowned airplane designer, designed the airplane. There were 99 ground volunteers that participated in the flight with weather, communications, fabrication, office staff, gift shop staff and more. Primarily individual contributions, and a few product equipment sponsors financed the Voyager. The project did not receive any government sponsorship.

When the airplane took off full of fuel, pilots and supplies, the gross takeoff weight was 9,694.5 pounds. The average altitude flown was about 11,000 feet. The Voyager took off from and landed at Edwards Air Force Base in California.

This milestone flight took 9 days, 3 minutes and 44 seconds. To this day, no aircraft has flown more air miles than the Voyager's 26,358 statute miles. Not even close.

Four days after landing, President Ronald Reagan presented the Voyager crew and its designer with the Presidential Citizenship Medal. Awarded only 16 times previously in history.

What is your favorite plane to fly?

My all-time favorite plane to fly would have to be the F-100 Super Sonic Jet I flew in the Air Force. That said, and although the flying qualities were abominable, the Voyager was my favorite plane. Not for how it flew, but for its challenges, what it represented and its success. It was also so rewarding to have an incredible team of nearly 100 volunteers helping us every inch of the way and believing and sharing in our dream.

What is one of your most memorable aviation experiences/moments?

We were nearing Edwards Air Base at the successful end of Voyager's world flight, I couldn't see a thing, there was a solid deck of clouds below us. I was hoping that Edwards tower would give us clearance to land, knowing what a busy flight test center they are. In fact, I was just hoping to be able to get a ride back to Mojave. Then, the cloud cover broke, and through the clouds, I saw tens of thousands of people waiting for our return! People and vehicles lined the dry lake bed, and I was amazed at the sight! Before we landed, we did a few low passes, first with the gear up, then we lowered the gear for landing. I wanted to take the time to thank the supporters for the help and belief in our 'impossible' dream. It's a sight and a moment I will never, ever forget.

What do you still have left to do in aviation?   What adventures await you?

As I reach the twilight of my life, my goal is to continue to inspire others, encourage them in their own dreams. I am fortunate to be able to continue traveling the world speaking to groups of every kind, sharing my dreams, successes and even disappointments. I remind them, as my mother reminded me, "You are only limited by what you can dream." And "The only way to fail is to quit."

How to Become a Flight Instructor

Twenty-one-year-old Casey Weaver tells us what it's like to be a flight instructor at Santa Monica Airport.

What inspired you to want to fly?

My dad took a few flight lessons. That sparked a big interest in me, but I'm the first pilot in my family. Even as a little kid, hopping on a commercial flight was fun. Taking off was my favorite part! When I started training, landing became my favorite part. I have always loved planes.

Is it hard to learn how to fly?

It can be. You have to apply yourself and really be committed to flying. Once you focus on the actual flying, flying is really just like anything else. It takes a lot of practice and planning.

How old were you when you started flying?

I started flying at 16 years old. I became a certified flight instructor when I was 21.

Do you still like to fly?

I do! I see something new every day. Whether it's a new pool or a brand-new landmark. Not only that, you learn something every time you fly.

Is it hard to teach people how to fly?

It's not hard but it requires work. It requires patience. Just like riding a bike, people sometimes take a little bit of time to get the hang of it. But once they do get it, it's very rewarding.

What is your favorite part of teaching people how to fly?

Seeing people progress is very rewarding. Seeing their faces light up when they understand a concept. Seeing someone go from not understanding what a plane is to flying it by themselves. It's very rewarding.

How long does it take to become an instructor?

There is no set amount of time. You become a pilot first and then you can become an instructor. Just like learning how to fly, it's about being really committed. Not only studying and learning the material, but flying. Flying itself is a big key to instructing. The more flight hours you have, the more you can actually understand what is going on in the air.

How many flight hours do you have in an airplane?

I have about 1,000 hours, 600 hundred of which have been spent teaching students. The next step is commercial flying, flying people to destinations, not teaching them, but flying them around.

How can I someday learn to fly?

Take an introductory/discovery flight and see if you like it. It's very low cost and very safe.

What is your favorite airport?

Santa Monica Airport! I like the way it's run, the tower, and using the runway is fun. My next favorite airport is Van Nuys Airport because of how big it is. Even though it's considered a "small airport" compared to LAX, Van Nuys is busier than ever!

The Last Airplane Builder at Santa Monica Airport

We caught up with Dave Ronneberg, the last aircraft builder at Santa Monica Airport, and asked him about his 30+ years working on the field.

Dave Ronneberg, builder of the Berkut aircraft. Image circa 2004.

Where did your parents meet?

My parents were both employees at the Douglas Aircraft Factory at Santa Monica Airport around 1944 and they met there. My father was bucking rivets on many of their aircraft (including the DC-3 and C-47).

What inspired you to start building airplanes?

When I was a kid I started building balsa wood airplanes and rockets as a hobby. I was fascinated with flight. My friends and I even tried to strap wings on our backs and get up enough speed on roller skates to "fly" in the driveway. I don't recommend that to kids these days!

Who is one of your aviation heroes?

I was fascinated by Charles Lindbergh as a kid. He flew from Long Island, NY to Paris in a single-engine plane called the Spirit of St. Louis.

What type of plane did you build?

I started my career building a plane called the "VariEze."

Then, Burt Rutan (a legendary aircraft designer) released plans for the "Long EZ" plane. I began building those for customers for many years.

Although the Long EZ was a terrific plane (and well-designed), I found some areas that I wanted to customize. I began working on plans for this evolved version of the plane and called it Berkut.

The Berkut didn't improve on the already excellent design of the Long EZ's wing sweep, wing sizes or airfoil choices. It did, however make a few small customizations to make it user friendly. Many of these improvements were "unblessed hints" customers had asked for over the years. I added retractable landing gear (designed by Shirland Dickey), a double canopy, bigger fuselage and a larger engine.

I built 77 kits of the Berkut that people could buy and assemble themselves.

Where do your Berkut planes fly?

My planes fly all over the world. They are currently in Switzerland, Great Britain, South Africa, Japan, Malta, Germany and the rest are in the U.S.

Part 4

100 Years of History at The Santa Monica Airport

Parents, this part of the book will tell you some of the great history of the Santa Monica Airport and the daring people who flew here. Many of these stories can be read out loud with your kids when you visit the locations described.

It All Started in 1917

Clover Field in 1922 looking northwest, with the City of Santa Monica and the bay in the distance. The street in the front of the picture is Centinela Avenue. Just two years after this picture was taken, the first planes to fly around the world would take off from this airport.

No one exactly knows who the first pilot was to take off and land in Santa Monica. People had been taking off and landing where Santa Monica Airport is now from as early as 1917, and maybe earlier. Before that it was mostly farmland.

After the end of World War I, around November of 1918, pilots who had flown during the war started flying their war surplus biplanes into Clover Field. It was possible then to buy a complete airplane—new in a crate—for $350. Some of these pilots flew for movies, some flew aerial displays to thrill the crowds, some taught others how to fly, and some did all three. Many modified their planes to fly faster and farther. They started flying races to set records and win glory and prize money.

Douglas Aircraft Company

Above: The third location of the Douglas Aircraft Company on Wilshire and 23rd Street (before they moved to Santa Monica Airport). This location is now called "Douglas Park" and is on the north side of Wilshire Blvd.

At about the same time, in 1922, the company that would soon make Santa Monica famous, the Douglas Aircraft Company, moved into their first big factory, an abandoned movie studio on Wilshire Boulevard and 23rd Street. Before that they had a small factory on Pico at 4th Street (near where Santa Monica High School is currently located). When Douglas moved to Wilshire, the company had 6 employees. By 1965 there would be 175,000 employees in different factories all over Los Angeles County.

Donald Douglas

Above: Donald Douglas decided he wanted to make airplanes after he saw the Wright brothers fly when he was a teenager. Here at his factory he holds sections of a wing he and his engineers designed. The cross section of the wings are similar to the shape of the wing shown earlier in the book.

Douglas' love of airplanes began in 1908 when he was 16 and convinced his mother he needed to watch as the Wright Brothers flew their trial flights for the U.S. government. He entered the Naval Academy at Annapolis in 1909. Three years later, he switched schools to MIT and finished their four-year aeronautical engineering degree in two years.

He found an investor, David R. Davis, who agreed to finance a plane that could fly coast to coast nonstop. The new company, the Davis-Douglas Company, had $40,000 and their first order for one airplane. It was called "The Cloudster."

The Cloudster first flew on Feb 24, 1921, and quietly accomplished a breakthrough in aviation: It was the very first airplane to lift not only its own weight (9,600 pounds), but also an additional, equal amount of weight (another 9,600 pounds). It could potentially fly mail and other important freight.

Davis, however was mainly interested in setting racing records. (The Cloudster did attempt the record but developed engine trouble halfway, so the flight was stopped. Instead, the first non-stop transcontinental record was set on May 2-3, 1923 by two U.S. Army Service pilots flying a Fokker T-2 from New York to San Diego in about 27 hours. It was their third attempt). Davis ultimately left the company, and Douglas continued on as the Douglas Aircraft Company.

In 1921, Douglas secured a commission from the Navy for a new folding-wing torpedo plane (the DT-1) and funding with the help of *L.A. Times* publisher Harry Chandler. By 1924, Douglas had moved his factory to the old Herman Film Corporation building on 24th and Wilshire in Santa Monica.

The Douglas Torpedo Plane #2 (DT-2), made on Wilshire, was sophisticated and very strong. It had a welded frame, made in 3 pieces for easy storage and repair, and could be configured with floats for water landings. The DT-2 was so successful that it became the basis for the Douglas World Cruiser, the first plane to fly all the way around the world.

Donald Douglas' aircraft company went on to build three different types of planes. Some would carry mail, others were Army cargo planes, some were medical evacuation planes. The company even made the first successful plane that could take off and land on water, the Douglas Dolphin.

Douglas also built observation planes for the military, and planes for civilians to fly. He and his employees carved out a little dirt airstrip behind their factory on Wilshire so pilots could take off and land there. Charles Lindberg flew in and out of the factory on Wilshire and 23rd. Lindberg was the last person fly out in and out of the Wilshire Boulevard factory before it closed in 1929 and Douglas moved the factory to the Santa Monica Airport.

The Douglas Torpedo (DT-3) plane was made at the factory on Wilshire in 1921. Ninety of these planes were made. These planes took off from a carrier and could drop torpedoes. They had floats for water landing. The floats are on in the plane in this picture above, but the whole plane is on a wheeled dolly so it could be moved around on dry land. You can see from the man standing on the left side of the picture how large the Torpedo plane really was.

By 1929 Douglas had moved out of the Wilshire plant to Santa Monica Airport. The Wilshire plant location is currently called "Douglas Park," a public park available for all to see and enjoy.

Donald Douglas would go on to make the Douglas Commercial planes and military planes during World War II. He was a manufacturer of genius and helped pioneer techniques to go from making aircraft a few at a time to creating them in mass quantities via production-line assembly. His company produced roughly 30,000 aircraft in just three years between 1942 and 1945. Douglas Aircraft grew from a small company of just 68 employees in 1922, into one of the top 10 largest businesses in the U.S. by 1965.

Little known facts about the neighborhood:

The name of the street on the east side of the airport is "Centinela," which comes from the Rancho Ajuaje de la Centinela. The Rancho was in the "Centinela Valley," roughly where Westchester, Inglewood and El Segundo are now. "Centinela" is the Spanish word for sentinel (to guard over or keep watch on flocks below). The Californio ranchers and shepherds stood on local hillsides and watched their animals graze down below. Before the Spanish came to California, the land was part of the lands of the Tongva People (for which the Tongva park in Santa Monica is named).

The Original Name: Clover Field

Before it was the Santa Monica Airport, it was called Clover Field.

The airfield in Santa Monica was dedicated as Clover Field on April 15, 1923 by the U.S. Army Air Corps, which had a hangar on the field. The airfield was dedicated to Lt. Greayer Clover, who grew up near the Westside and was killed in action during WWI. Fifty thousand people attended the dedication, and a formation flight of all available aircraft in Southern California flew over and landed at the newly dedicated field.

Greayer Clover graduated in 1915 from Los Angeles High School on Olympic Blvd. He attended Stanford and then Yale before enlisting. When he was killed in action four months before the end of the war, his grieving high school friends petitioned the government to have the airfield named in his honor. The students

Lt. Greayer Clover, the namesake for Clover Field (the name before Santa Monica Airport).

also raised $20,000 (an extraordinary amount of money at the time) to buy the land across the street from L.A. High School. They put up a building to serve as a memorial to Clover and the other L.A. High School students killed in the war. This building still stands, it is now the Memorial Branch Library, (a public library), and can be visited at 4625 W. Olympic Boulevard. Clover Avenue, Clover Avenue Elementary School and Cloverfield Boulevard also have names dedicated to Greayer Clover. The library even has a large wall with stained glass windows—which can still be seen today—dedicated to Lt. Clover and 19 of his fallen classmates.

The World Cruisers (1924)

The First Flight Around the World Started and Ended at Santa Monica Airport

This is Clover Field in 1924. It was re-named Santa Monica Airport three years later in 1927. This picture was taken the day the World Cruisers started their record-breaking flight around the world.

The World Cruisers were built at the Douglas factory on Wilshire. They were based on the DT-3 Torpedo Planes Douglas made for the Navy. The World Cruisers were put on trucks and brought down to Clover Field where three of them took off on April 24, 1924. They were the very first planes to fly all the way around the world. (Two of the planes made it the whole distance; all the pilots lived to tell their tales). The World Cruisers flew at about the speed a car drives on the freeway today, 65 to 75 miles an hour.

They were cloth, open cockpit biplanes, 14 feet tall, weighing 4,000 pounds, about double the size of today's single-engine airplanes. They flew 28,945 miles through freezing and tropical conditions, through 33 countries on four continents. When they returned to Santa Monica six month later on September 23, 1924, a crowd of 200,000 people came out to meet them. Newspapers all over the world wrote about the planes during their long trip.

People from countries near and far then learned about Santa Monica, and that it was a place where you came to build and fly planes.

Above: September 23, 1924, the day the World Cruisers came home.

You Could Fly All Around Los Angeles

In the early days, there were over 60 airfields all over Los Angeles.

Behold the corner of Wilshire and Fairfax in 1919. The famous movie director Cecil B. DeMille owned this airfield (and two others in Los Angeles). He operated Mercury Aviation and flew 2,500 passengers in four years of operation. The planes in the photograph would have also landed at Santa Monica, as Mercury Aviation made frequent stops there.

There were around 65 airports in greater Los Angeles in the 1920s and 1930s. If you could afford it, you could easily get around by air. Most cars travelled about 25 to 30 miles an hour, and even if your car went faster, the roads could be rough and the freeways would not exist for another 30 years. The excellent street car system was available, but the street cars did not necessarily go everywhere people needed to go. So, people got around by airplane (or horseback. Twenty years after this picture was taken, you could still ride your horse from Compton to Pasadena and back).

Above: Producer/Director Cecil B. DeMille's airfield on the northeast corner of Wilshire and Fairfax. Note the Cahuenga pass in the distance.
Below: Charlie Chaplin's field on the southwest corner of Wilshire and Fairfax, across the street from DeMille's field.

The Venice Airport

Above: Aerial photo of Ince Field in Venice on Washington Blvd. Note the Grand Canal in the lower right of the image. Abbot Kinney built the canals to attract people to his city "Venice of America."

During the teens, the busiest airfield in the area was not the airstrip at Santa Monica. It was the Ince Aviation Field located along Venice Boulevard at Abbot Kinney. It became an official airfield in 1913 and was named by the silent movie producer Thomas Ince who owned both the land and the airfield operation.

Venice's airport (the Ince Aviation Field) was located at the intersection of Abbot Kinney and Venice Blvd, 1913.

Ince was a pioneer of motion picture production. He was a producer, one of the early filmmakers to shoot "out of sequence" to maximize his work day, getting the most out of the daylight hours and keeping several shoots going simultaneously. He made mostly Westerns, shooting in his enormous 7.5-mile-long backlot called "Inceville" located in Santa Ynez Canyon, reaching up from the end of Sunset Boulevard into the Palisades Highlands.

In 1919, Ince offered $50,000 dollars of his own money in an Aero Club of America-sanctioned race for "anyone who could complete the first aerial voyage across the Pacific Ocean in a heavier-than-air machine, mechanically propelled, of any size and type. Any westward-headed flight must start at Ince Aviation Field in Venice, California or the Thomas H. Ince Hydroaeroplane Station (the location of which is unfortunately no longer

A wing walker flying over Pickering Pier in 1922 in Venice Beach, CA.

known), also in Venice." The prize money was never claimed. Ince himself was out of the picture by 1920, having met an untimely, non-aviation-related death.

The signage painted on his hangar was left up out of loyalty to him by the man who took over, a stunt pilot of great daring and skill named Beverly DeLay. DeLay had managed the field for Ince. He had also acted in and flown for studios such as Pathé, Warner Brothers, Fox and Universal among many others. By the early 1920s, DeLay and his crew of pilots at DeLay Field not only flew stunts but taught stunt flying. DeLay Field was the center for motion picture aviation, with a skilled and daring group of stunt pilots flying in and out of the field. Some of the most daring and elaborate aerial stunts were dreamed up in the field's hangers, and motion picture cameramen were often on hand to film them.

A businessman named Abbot Kinney, meanwhile, seized the opportunity to promote his real-estate brainchild, the canals at

Venice of America. He had a keen sense of promotion and knew how to please the large crowds that flocked to the beach looking for fun in the evening. Kinney hired pilots to fly exhibition flights in the skies over and adjacent to the canals at what would eventually be known simply as Venice, today one of Los Angeles' most colorful residential, commercial and recreational beachfront neighborhoods.

Stunts, daring aircraft-to-aircraft leaps (tamely called "transfers"), and exhibition parachuting were part of the fun, and given the competitive natures of the pilots and their ever-growing skills, these displays developed into nighttime aerial stunt performances—aerobatics over the dark ocean in cloth Curtis "Jenny" biplanes with blazing magnesium flares strapped to their wing tips. It would be hard to overstate the hazards involved, but the crowds were thrilled.

These nighttime takeoffs and landings may have been on a lit field, lights provided by the Ince studios. **If so, Ince Field/DeLay Field on Venice Boulevard may have been the world's first lit airfield.** It could also be safe to assume that since Santa Monica had an Army presence at the field through the late teens and '20s, Ince Field in Venice—without any Army supervision—may have been the more desirable choice of the two airfields for the most daring and adventurous stunt pilots.

Beverly DeLay's airplane was later sabotaged, possibly in a dispute over the land. The land was sold and the airfield was dismantled in 1923. Most of the stunt pilots moved their hangars to Clover Field, eventually resuming flying. Clover Field became busier than ever.

In April 1919, Venice became the first city in America with an aerial police force. The owner of this 100-mile-per-hour biplane (left) was sworn in as a deputy by Venice's Chief of Police. The pilot, with plane, was stationed at Ince Airfield. There he would be reached by telephone to follow fleeing suspects or locate boats in distress. Also, the new police air unit was splendid publicity for the city.

The Story of Abbot Kinney and Venice of America

In 1891, Mr. Abbot Kinney and a partner owned all the land from Ocean Park, Santa Monica to Marina del Rey. They began building a city in Ocean Park, including roads, homes, hotels and an amusement pier. Ocean Park was good, stable land. South of Ocean Park, though, it was mostly "swamp" land.

When Kinney's partner was replaced, the new partner didn't share Kinney's vision. To sever the partnership and split the parcel they agreed to toss a coin.

Kinney won the coin toss, and chose the swamp. His partner said: "See, I told you he was crazy!"

But Abbot Kinney had a grander vision for creating a unique community by the sea: he dredged the wetlands to create canals, built Venetian architecture, a salt water plunge, a dance hall, piers, wild amusement rides, and much more. It was called

"Venice of America," Kinney's mash-up of Venice, Italy and Coney Island. Source: VenicePublicArt.com and Wikepedia.org

From 1905 to 1929, the area covered by canals was approximately three times as large as today. The entire area between Abbot Kinney, Pacific, and Venice Blvd. were canals.

Above: Two women dive into canals that are now paved roadways. Behind them is tiny United States Island. (Image: Security Pacific National Bank Collection - Los Angeles Public Library)

Below: The main lagoon at Venice of America. This intersection is now near Windward Ave and Grand Ave, current location of the old Post Office in Venice. Circa 1918 (Image: Unknown)

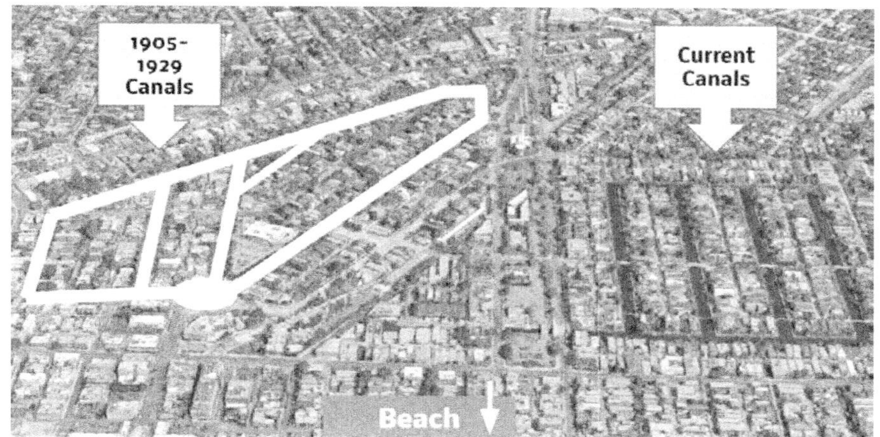

Above: Abbot Kinney 's canals covered almost three times as much surface area in 1905-1929. The large circle is now the traffic loop infront of the old Venice Post Office.

Abbot Kinney's success at promoting his development brought thousands of people to Venice of America. Unfortunately, as they began to move to Venice, the land became more expensive, making Venice airfield attractive to develop as apartments and homes. The closing of DeLay Field shifted the focus of local flyers and aviation businesses to Clover Field in Santa Monica.

Clover Field becomes Santa Monica Airport

Clover Field 1924 looking Northeast. (Image: SMGov.net)

In 1926 the city of Santa Monica purchased the parcel of land called Clover Field for $755,000.

On June 15th, 1927, the Santa Monica City Council changed the name of Clover Field to Santa Monica Airport.

It's an interesting note that the airport was only officially called Clover Field from 1923-1927 (four short years) however, many aviators still refer to the airport (and are very fond of that name) even to this day.

Above: A photo in of Albert P. "Al" Wilson, a Hollywood movie stunt pilot with his airplane, flying over Santa Monica Airport on February 29, 1928. Al Wilson was a flight instructor and taught Cecil B. DeMille how to fly (at DeLay field in Venice, Ca). Later he would manage Cecil's business, the Mercury Aviation Company. "Al" Wilson was a charter member of the AMPP, the Associated Motion Picture Pilots, the stunt pilots' union founded by Pancho Barnes in 1931.

The Women's Air Derby of 1929

Left: From the left of the photo are: Pancho Barnes, Elizabeth McQueen (an early supporter of women's aviation activities), Amelia Earhart, Santa Monica Pilot Clema Granger, Elizabeth Kelly Inwood, Gladys O'Donnell (in helmet and goggles) Janet Roberts, Mildred Morgan and Valentine Sprague. **Right:** Pilot Ruth Elder

In August 1929, pioneering women pilots flew in the first Women's Air Derby. Big air races had been held since 1909, but women pilots had not been allowed to enter the races. The Women's Air Derby was then established. It was part of the 1929 National Air Races and Aeronautical Exposition. In August of 1929, fewer than 2,000 Americans held pilot licenses, and only seventy were women. Twenty women came to Santa Monica Airport and started the race—eighteen from the U.S. and one each from Australia (Jessie Keith-Miller) and Germany (Thea Rasche). Among the entrants was Amelia Earhart in her first competitive race, and the accomplished pilot Pancho Barnes.

Using road maps like you would have in a car, they flew the 2,700-mile race from Santa Monica to Cleveland, stopping in Arizona, New Mexico, Texas, Oklahoma, Kansas, Missouri, Illinois and Indiana. The race took nine days and brought global attention to women aviators and to Santa Monica Airport.

Three Air Derby Racers Arrive Within Days and Sign the SMO Register
(Airports used to have registers, like guest books, where pilots would sign in
when they landed, but airports don't have these anymore)

Mary von Mach, Marvel Crosson and Edith Foltz all arrived at Santa
Monica Airport within days of each other to compete in the 1929 Air
Derby. At the time of the race, Mary von Mach was one of only two
licensed pilots in Michigan. Marvel Crosson was the first woman to
receive her pilot's license in Alaska. Edith Foltz was the first woman to
receive her pilot's license in Oregon.

Above Left: Many of the female pilots of the 1929 Women's Air Derby.
Above Right: Louise Thaden, Gladys O'Connell and Ruth Nichols, pilots who flew
the first women's U.S. transcontinental Air Derby. The race started at the Santa
Monica Airport. Louise Thaden won the race. (Image: Saint Louis University
Library). At the time of this race, there was no FAA (Federal Aviation
Administration) to issue pilot's licenses. Instead the licenses were issued by the
French-based Fédération Aéronautique Internationale, or FAI, the organization
that still sanctions and authenticates all world aviation records).

Louise Thaden signed the Santa Monica Airport Register

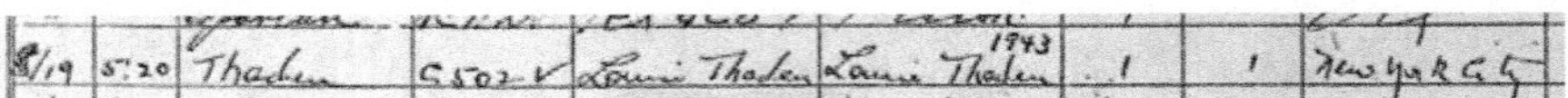

Louise Thaden flew into Santa Monica Airport on August 19th, 1931 two years to the day after she had taken off from Santa Monica to win the Women's Air Derby in 1929. Thaden was not among the participants that signed the register on the day of the original Derby from Santa Monica to Cleveland. In that race, Thaden defeated Amelia Earhart and other top women pilots to win $25,000 in the heavy class.

Blanche Noyes signed the Santa Monica Airport Register

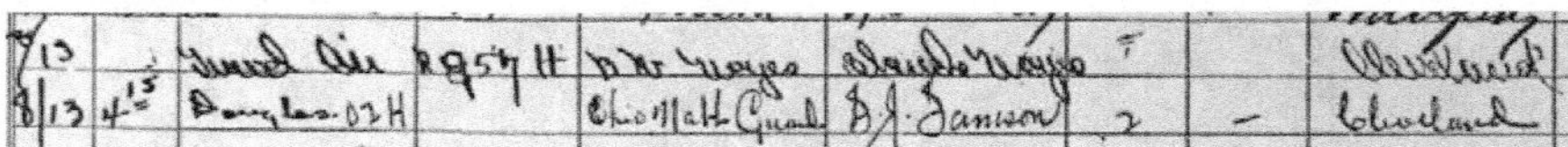

Blanche Noyes flew into Santa Monica on August 13th, 1929, 5 days before the start of the Women's Air Derby, flying from Cleveland to Santa Monica. Blanche Noyes was the first licensed female pilot in Ohio and perhaps the Cleveland National Guard Douglas 02H, which appears in the registry directly under her entry, was sent in her honor. During the race, she stated she "narrowly escaped death when her plane caught fire in mid-air near Pecos." She set down so hard her landing gear was damaged, but put out the fire, made repairs and resumed the race. She placed fourth in the heavy class.

Pancho Barnes: Female Stunt Pilot

Above: Pancho and her Travel Air Type R Mystery ship. Pancho crashed in the 1929 Women's Air Derby but returned to enter the race the very next year—and won, breaking Amelia Earhart's world women's speed record at 196.19 miles per hour. She broke the record flying a Travel Air Type R Mystery Ship with the sponsorship of Union Oil.

Pancho Barnes was an air racer, cross-country record setter, aerobatic pilot, adventurer and Hollywood stunt pilot. She flew faster than Amelia Earhart and at one point was "the fastest woman in the world," setting records in what was then the fastest civilian airplane in the world. She befriended artists and writers, movie stars and directors, and later in life was the drinking buddy of Chuck Yeager and the pilots of the early supersonic age.

She was born Florence Lowe Barnes to socialite parents in Pasadena. Her grandfather, Thaddeus S. C. Lowe, made a fortune in real estate and patents. He was an early pioneer of aviation, an "aeronaut"—an expert balloonist. He established America's first military air unit, a hot air aerial reconnaissance balloon corps during the Civil War.

Above: Glenn Curtiss flies a demonstration flight in his airplane "the June Bug" at the famous 1910 Los Angeles International Air Meet at Dominguez Field north of Long Beach. 200,000 people attended the two week long event.

When Pancho was 10, she and her grandfather went to the famous 1910 Los Angeles International Air Meet. The first major air meet in America was held at the Rancho of the Dominguez Family located north of Long Beach near the city of Carson, California. Two hundred and fifty thousand people attended the event, which lasted ten days. It was the first aviation meet in America. The Pacific Electric Railway company expanded rail service for the quarter of a million people who attended. While attending this event, Pancho's grandfather told her that someday she would be able to fly. She believed him.

Efforts to turn Pancho into a Pasadena debutante failed. Dressed like a man, she boarded a freighter for Mexico during the Mexican Revolution. The boat was later seized by pirates and held hostage for six week. Only the boat's helmsman and Pancho were brave enough to escape. Once ashore, they stole a horse and burro and traveled across Mexico.

She took the name Pancho so as not to draw the attention of the authorities. The name stuck. They walked and rode from Mexico City to Vera Cruz before stowing away on boats to New Orleans. On foot, hopping freight trains and hitch-hiking, they made it back to California. This was a grand adventure for Pancho, one of many to come.

In spring, 1928, she started taking flying lessons. Her instructor was a World War I pilot. The airplane's only instrument: an oil gauge. A keychain hung loose from the instrument panel to show their angle of bank, and she looked over the side to judge her altitude.

But in an instant, Pancho loved flying. She soloed after six hours of lessons, bought a Travel Air biplane for $5,500 and looked for opportunities to make money. She flew into towns and did aerial displays, and became a test pilot for airplane builders, flight-testing planes right off the factory floor. She also flew promotional flights for the Union Oil Company.

Pancho Barnes signed the Santa Monica Airport Register

Pancho Barnes landed at SMO in her Travel Air on May 7th, 1929. Here she signs in as "Florence Barnes" her legal name. The header of the Santa Monica Airport Register is included for reference.

On Feb 22, 1929, Pancho entered the first recorded women's pylon race, which was held at the Glendale, California, Grand Central Airport. The course was two laps from the field in Glendale, then to Metropolitan Airport in Van Nuys and return. Pancho easily won the 80-mile race by more than 24 minutes. She then beat several men racing from San Francisco to Los Angeles. She was hooked, but very few races were open to women until the Women's Air Derby of 1929. This transcontinental race from Santa Monica to Cleveland became the most prestigious race of the decade. Pancho did well in the early part of the race, finishing among the first three in each leg of the race. But in Pecos, Texas, a truck collided with her plane on the runway. Her plane was seriously damaged. She had to withdraw from the race.

In 1930, she returned to win the Women's Air Derby, shattering Earhart's speed record of 184.6 miles an hour by racing to 196.16 miles an hour in her Mystery Ship, easily one of the finest airplanes of the time. In 1931, the governor of California awarded her a trophy that proclaimed her "America's fastest woman flyer." She became Lockheed's first female test pilot.

She also worked in the ever-expanding film industry as a stunt pilot, stunt designer and technical aerial advisor. Pancho flew for Howard Hughes, capturing authentic audio of planes for his movie *Hell's Angels,* by, in a difficult maneuver, flying around tethered balloons with sound equipment attached to them. In 1931, she founded the Associated Motion Picture Pilots, the AMPP, a union that professionalized stunt flying by promoting safety, setting standards and regulating pay.

By August 30, 1939, Pancho signs in as Pancho, flying in to Santa Monica Airport from Glendale. The entry above at 9:30 is also interesting. That airplane is owned by Hal Roach, movie director and producer best known for his films starring Laurel and Hardy.

Amelia Earhart's Flight Instructor: Neta Snook

Neta Snook's early love of machines started with her parents' car. As a small child, Neta's father let her steer the car up and down the hills of their little town. At nine, Neta and her dad would study the car's instruction manual and learn about auto maintenance.

Neta went to college and took more than the required load of classes she had to take so she could take classes she really cared about—mechanical drawing, combustion engines, and a course in the repair, maintenance and overhaul of farm tractors. Reading about balloons and airplanes in the college library, she became convinced she wanted to fly. She applied to the Curtiss-Wright aviation school and was denied admission, her application stamped: "No females allowed." Early in 1917 Neta saw a notice in a Des Moines newspaper for a new flying school in Davenport, Iowa. It read, "Davenport Flying School—competent instructors—superb equipment. We guarantee to teach anybody to learn to fly for only $400."

Neta enrolled in the Davenport Flying School, located in an abandoned warehouse on the riverfront. The *"superb equipment"* described in the ad did not exist. Instead, the students had to build their airplane, which they constructed with wooden spars covered with linen. They covered the linen with seven coats of fabric sealer before crisscross steel cables tightened by turnbuckles held the plane together.

During World War I, she worked for the British Air Ministry in Elmira, New York. She inspected and tested aircraft engines bound for combat in Europe. After the war, she brought a wrecked Canadian "Canuck" (Curtis JN-4 Jenny) plane to her home, rebuilt it, soloed and got her license. Her pilot's license read the number of passengers she could carry as "none," so she erased the "n" to read "one." She took passengers on flights over the town, barnstormed the country and flew aerial advertising.

Ice and snow in the Midwest made flying impossible. In the fall of 1920, she dismantled her plane and shipped it to California. She then became a licensed flight instructor and became the first woman to run a commercial airfield, Kinner Field, in what is now South Gate. Sam Kinner made airplanes at his factory on the field.

Neta's skills as a mechanic made her invaluable. Other business at Kinner Field included passenger carrying, aerial advertising and flight instruction.

In 1921, Amelia Earhart, along with her father, walked onto the airfield and asked Neta, "I want to fly. Will you teach me?" The agreement between Amelia and her parents had been that only a woman pilot would teach her. Neta Snook taught Amelia Earhart to fly, and they became good friends.

Above: Flight instructor Neta Snook with student pilot Amelia Earhart at Kinner Field, South Gate, California in 1921. Neta received her FAI pilot's license in 1920. Earhart, Neta's student, received her FAI pilot's license in 1923, becoming the 16th woman to do so.

Amelia Earhart: The Long Distance Flyer

Amelia Earhart stands in front of her Lockheed Electra. Amelia Earhart did not begin flying until she moved to California in 1920 at age 23. The Electra was made in Burbank by the Lockheed Company.

Amelia Earhart was not the first woman pilot. (Baroness Raymonde de Laroche of France was the first woman to solo, in 1909, and in 1910 the first to earn a pilot's license), nor was she the first licensed woman pilot in America (that was Harriet Quimby in 1911), but Amelia Earhart is the best remembered.

Amelia Earhart was born in Atchison, Kansas, on July 24, 1897, a member of a railroad family. Her father was a railroad attorney, and her family moved where he went, so she grew up in a string of different railroad towns. Amelia had a strong sense of adventure, climbing trees, hunting with a rifle and speeding on her sled downhill. She dreamed of a non-traditional career, making scrap books about women in what were the mostly male-dominated fields of law, advertising, film direction/production, and mechanical engineering. At eleven, she saw her first airplane at the Iowa State fair in 1908.

Later at an aircraft fair in her early 20s, she and a friend watched as a World War I pilot dove his plane toward them, attempting to startle them. Earhart stood her ground. She later remarked, "I did not understand it at the time, but I believe that little red airplane said something to me as it swished by."

At 21, she felt compelled to leave school. She took courses in Red Cross First Aid and enlisted as a nurse's aide in a military hospital in Toronto, Canada, tending to wounded soldiers and aviators injured in World War I. In 1918, she enrolled as a pre-med student at Columbia University in New York.

When her parents moved to California, she joined them. In December 1920, Amelia went to an air show at Long Beach and for five dollars took her first airplane ride. "By the time I had got two or three hundred feet off the ground, I knew I had to fly," she later recalled.

On January 3, 1921 Amelia and her father went to Kinner Field (in what is now South Gate, California). Amelia asked flight instructor Neta Snook if she would teach her how to fly, and a friendship was born. In July 1921 with the help of her mother and sister, Amelia raised the deposit to buy the plane she first flew, the prototype Kinner Airster, for $2,000. It was a bright yellow biplane. She named it "the Canary."

The Canary was underpowered, but it could provide her with valuable flight time. In October 22, 1922, Amelia flew her plane to 14,000 feet (the highest altitude at which the aircraft could sustain level flight), setting a female world record for high altitude.

This is the first of many records she set. In 1928 she was the first woman to fly across the Atlantic, as a passenger. This made her famous, but she was not meant to be just along for the ride. Two years later she made the flight herself, soloing across the Atlantic, becoming in 1932 the first woman to do so. She was awarded the Distinguished Flying Cross award (a military decoration awarded for heroic achievement). In 1935 she became the first person to fly solo across the Pacific from Honolulu to Oakland, **making Amelia Earhart the first person to solo anywhere in the Pacific, and the first person to solo across both the Atlantic and the Pacific.**

Two years after her solo across the Pacific, Amelia and her navigator, Fred Noonan, started their attempted around-the-world-flight taking off from Miami eastward. After completing 22,000 miles of their flight, they were last seen taking off from Lae, New Guinea on July 2nd, 1937. It was not just the records she set, but the records she aimed at, for which she would be remembered.

Above: May 20, 1932 – Amelia Earhart becomes the first woman to make a solo flight across the North Atlantic.

Below: July 1936 – Amelia walks in front of her Lockheed L-10E Electra.

The Airport in the 1930s

Above: Santa Monica Airport in 1929. Sixty-three acres were added to the Eastern part of the field (bottom of photo), and the runway was a total of 2,800 feet long. The street at the bottom of the photo is Centinela. In future years, the city will expand the runway, and Centinela will curve East to connect with Bundy.

In 1933, Santa Monica Airport was a very professional, well-equipped airport that any city would be proud of, and Santa Monica was very proud of its airport. By then the airport was known all over the world.

The airport was a 63-acre rectangle with a 2,800-foot paved asphalt runway. Daytime markings at Clover Field were the standard circle at the center of the field and "CLOVER FIELD" painted in enormous letters on a hangar. At night, it had a green, rotating beacon, with boundary and flood lights. There were no landing fees, and no flood lighting fees for night landings.

This is a view of the airport in 1931 looking east. Although it was named Santa Monica Airport in 1927, the hangar on the left in the photo still reads "Clover Field." The large building on the left is the Douglas Aircraft Company.

Douglas Aircraft Company, which manufactured aircraft under contract for the Army, Navy, Coast Guard and foreign governments, was also at Santa Monica. Its facility is the large, flat-roofed structure on the far left of the picture.

Wrigley Family Landed at Santa Monica Airport in a Douglas Plane

The Wrigley Family-owned Douglas Dolphin arrived in Santa Monica from Avalon on 5/27/1935. Catalina Island was once owned by William Wrigley, Jr. of Wrigley chewing gum fame. Wrigley developed Avalon as a resort island destination and often brought the Chicago Cubs baseball team (which he owned) to the Island for spring training. The wheeled, but also amphibious, Douglas Dolphin would have been the perfect aircraft to fly from the bay at Avalon to the field at Santa Monica.

Communication equipment at the field consisted of a telephone (number was 83966), and weather reports. Local accommodations were first rate. There were modern hotels in the city and a restaurant on the field. Buses ran every 20 minutes, and taxi fare to town was 50 cents.

Service facilities were also excellent. Gas, oil and hangars were available, as were complete repair facilities, with licensed mechanics on call day or night.

Santa Monica Airport circa 1933. (Image: Granger)

Learn to fly at Santa Monica Airport—the 1930s way

Above: Jim Granger with his first OX-5 JN4D2 Jenny. (Image: Granger)
Below: Clema Granger. Her pilot's license was signed by Orville Wright.

Jim and Clema Granger bought this airplane in 1926 for $350. The plane came in its original crate as war surplus. Jim trucked it to Clover Field from Ontario, California and hired well-known air racer (and fellow operator at the Santa Monica Airport) Kenneth Montee to teach him to fly it. Jim and Clema promptly opened "Granger's, Incorporated" at Clover Field. By 1928 Jim had changed the name to "Pacific School of Aviation."

Clema Granger learned to fly at Santa Monica in 1929. Orville Wright signed her license. She flew in the Air Derbies of 1930, 1931 and 1932, performed aerial stunts, and later was treasurer of

the 99s (an organization of women pilots) during the years when
Amelia Earhart was its president.

Clema Granger signed the Santa Monica Airport Register

Clema Granger signed the register on May 9th, 1930. She flew a
Swallow, an English made airplane on a flight originating from the
Culver City Airport arriving at Santa Monica. The Culver City Airport was
near Sepulveda Boulevard and Jefferson Boulevard (at the intersection
of the 90 and 405 freeways); it was closed in 1951 and turned into an
apartment complex.

She and Jim taught their three sons how to fly by the time each
was 16. "The Flying Grangers" performed and flew stunts for films.

This is what people were doing in airplanes in Los Angeles in the 1920s. Stunt
pilots often shunned parachutes to get better footage on screen, to increase
thrills and as a show of trust. Stunt woman Gladys Ingle (shown above) a
member of the "13 Black Cats", performed an astounding 310 airplane-to-
airplane transfers without a parachute. Gladys Ingle died in 1981, at age 82.

Many of the first licensed pilots and famous early Los Angeles
aviators were actors and actresses. Director Cecil B. DeMille not
only flew, he owned airports from Altadena to Mid-Wilshire, flying

passengers all over the state. Charlie Chaplin and his brother/manager Sydney operated an airfield. Mary Pickford owned an airplane. Rudolf Valentino, director William Wellman and many others flew and also performed their own stunts. The worlds of the pilot, actor and director converged, often into the same individual. United by a love of excitement and the freedom of flying (as well as the money required to do it), these artists put the movie camera right on the airplane, showing audiences the world from the sky with speed and thrilling realism they'd never seen before. Fans flocked to watch their heroes perform in person, and actors performed flying tours to promote their films.

Stunt pilots and aerial acts flew from local airports, mainly DeLay field in Venice, then Santa Monica. The "13 Black Cats"—named to show their defiance of superstition—had a hangar at Santa Monica.

Jim Granger signed the Santa Monica Airport Register

Jim Granger signed on May 16th, 1930 at 2:55 pm, his flight originating at Wichita, Kansas arriving at Cloverfield. Jim and Clema Granger had a flight school on the field at Santa Monica Airport. Note Jim's charming, tiny comment about his flight, "Nice Trip ask Nick."

Above: Circa 1934. The wing-walking biplane aerial stunt troop named the "13 Black Cats" flew out of Santa Monica after DeLay Field in Venice closed.

Below: Santa Monica Airport, December 1, 1934. Aerial photo looking east and north. The Douglas Facility is the large, flat-roofed building on the left. By now Douglas Aircraft is a big, busy operation.

1939-40 (Before WWII)

Above: March 1939 - In an advertisement from 1939, the caption reads "Here, in the center of America's greatest flying activity, 55% of the nation's planes are engineered, designed and built." (Image: Popular Aviation)

Below: The Douglas Aircraft plant at 3000 Ocean Park Blvd in 1940. By the time this photo had been taken, the DC-3 had been manufactured here and been flying for over 5 years.

Howard Hughes

Above: Howard Hughes with his H-1 Racer, NR258Y.

Young Howard Hughes

Howard R. Hughes Jr., pilot, designer, manufacturer, film director, producer and genius real estate entrepreneur was born on Dec 24th 1905 in Humble, Texas, just outside of Houston. At 14, Hughes began flying biplanes. When he was 18, his father died, and the young Hughes (whose mother had died two years earlier) found himself majority owner of the very successful Hughes Tool Company founded by Howard Sr., an innovative manufacturer of oil drilling equipment in oil-rich Texas.

When Howard was 20 in 1926, he began investing part of his profits into Hollywood films. He produced some of the quality movies of the 1920's and 1930's— *The Front Page*, *Two Arabian Knights* and *Scarface*. But his direction and production of *Hell's Angels* in 1930 secured his reputation in the film industry. The film's technical innovations changed moviemaking. Its spectacular aerial action sequences were a hit, and the shrewd casting of lovely Jean Harlow in her first starring role made the film a winner. At the time, Hughes was just 28.

Hughes obtained his first pilot's license in January 1928, after taking lessons at the Santa Monica airport.

(He kept a hangar at Santa Monica until the 1970s.) In 1932, the young millionaire Hollywood director suddenly left Hollywood. Under the assumed name of Charles Howard, and telling no one, he took a job paying $250 a month as a copilot with American Airways. He stayed long enough to learn what he wanted to learn about commercial aviation—about two months—and then left the job to embark on his new goal: To become the designer, builder and test pilot of high-performance aircraft and innovator of their specialized systems.

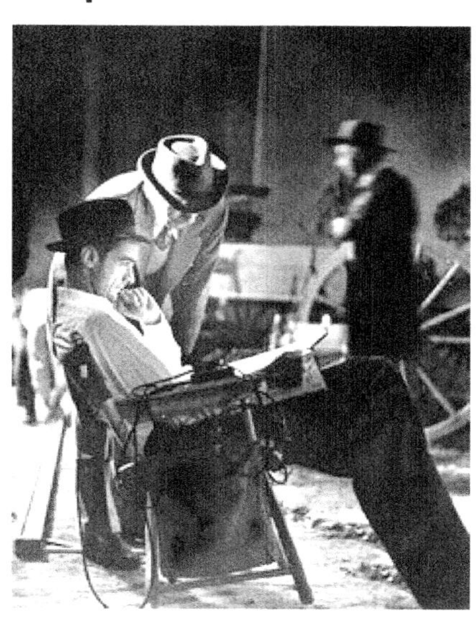

Above: Howard Hughes studying the script on the movie set for 'The Outlaw,' Hollywood, 1943 (Image: Life)

In 1932 he founded Hughes Aircraft Company in Glendale, California. In 1935, flying an airplane of his own design, he broke the world's speed record and was forced to crash land. In 1936 he broke the transcontinental speed record. In 1937 he beat his own record, flying even faster. In 1938, with a crew of four, he flew around the world in the record-breaking time of just over 91 hours. (Fourteen years earlier, the Douglas World Cruisers had taken six months to fly around the world.) Hughes was a hero, honored with parades and a congressional medal.

The Hughes Tool Company he had inherited, meanwhile, continued its financial success throughout the 1930s and during World War II. In 1939, he bought control of Trans World Airlines (TWA), the passenger airline. Hughes revolutionized the passenger travel industry when he used his tool company to buy a fleet of brand new Lockheed airliner that could travel from New York to Los Angeles in ten hours.

1n 1941, Hughes moved his factory from Glendale to the large factory he built at Centinela Ave and Jefferson near Culver City (the current site of Playa Vista condos and apartments). His factory had its own runway, which at almost two miles long was the largest privately owned runway in the world. There Hughes designed and built the Hercules, still the largest plane ever flown.

Nicknamed the "Spruce Goose," the plane took 5 years to build. It was built in the largest wooden building in the world (which as of print is still standing in the Playa Vista neighborhood at 5865 S. Campus Center Drive). The Hercules was finished in 1947 after the end of World War II. It was flown just once, by Hughes himself, over the water off Long Beach, but the research for the Hercules was invaluable in the development of the airliners yet to be built.

Howard Hughes inside the Spruce Goose

During the war, Hughes Aircraft was an important government contractor, developing and patenting a flexible feed for the speedier loading of machine guns on B-17 bombers. Their drives for machine guns to help reduce the incidence of gun jams. Hughes manufactured more ammunition belts than any other American manufacturer (Building Victory by Dana T. Parker). Hughes built 6,370 rear fuselage sections and 5,576 wings for Vultee BT-13 trainers.

Howard Hughes signed the Santa Monica Airport Register

Howard Hughes signed into the Santa Monica Airport register on April 27, 1929. He writes that his plane is owned by the "Caddo Company," his production company, which produced several Academy Award nominated films in the 1920s and 1930s. Hughes took flying instruction at the Santa Monica Airport, after which he received his private pilot's license.

One year before he flew the Hercules, Howard completed and flew a plane he designed, the XF-11 experimental reconnaissance plane. He crashed into a house at the edge of a golf course in Beverly Hills. He was not expected to live. But he did, and went on to successfully fly the XF-11 one year later and go on to finish and fly the Hercules/Spruce Goose. (A tireless innovator, while stuck in his hospital bed Hughes designed the motorized hospital bed so patients could more easily sit up.)

The innovations Howard Hughes and his companies pioneered are legend, but when a reporter asked him why he did his own test flying instead of simply hiring a test pilot, the answer

Howard Hughes in the cockpit of the first prototype XF-11, with all propellers turning, at Culver City, California.
(Image: UNLV Libraries)

was pure Howard Hughes: "Why should someone else have all the fun?"

The War Years

Above: The Douglas Aircraft Company factory is covered with a fake neighborhood to be hidden from enemy aircraft. Circa 1942.

Keeping an Airport Secret and Hidden in Plain Site

Well, the airport was almost a secret. People living in Santa Monica knew it was there, the Women's Auxiliary Ferry Squadron (WAFs), and Women Army Service Pilots (WASPs) who flew the planes on the runway painted to look like corn fields knew the airport was there, and the Douglas employees certainly knew it was there. But because of the war—hoping to protect it from becoming a bombing target—the airport and factory were made to disappear.

The idea came one day in 1939, when Donald Douglas was sailing on his boat out on Santa Monica Bay. (Douglas loved the ocean. He had gone to the Naval Academy at Annapolis until he decided to study aeronautical engineering at MIT.)

Enjoying the day, Douglas looked to shore and saw metal buildings gleaming in the sun, visible for miles. He thought briefly, pleasantly, "There's my factory!" Then it hit him. His factory was a great big shiny target.

Bombers had devastated parts of Europe, especially targeting rail lines, food production—and factories. Douglas immediately decided to camouflage his factory. He contacted respected local architect H. Roy Kelley, (inventor of the split-level ranch house) and landscape architect Edward Huntsman-Trout, to create plans.

Major John Ohmer had a similar idea. Fascinated by the problems of camouflage, in 1938 Ohmer formed the 604th Engineers Battalion, a camouflage unit of the 4th Army. He recruited a reserve auxiliary of Hollywood filmmakers, cinematographers, scenic designers, art directors, landscape artists, set builders, painters and animators from Columbia, Warner Brothers, MGM and other studios. Ohmer had access to the best theatrical designers and large-scale scenic artists in the world and put them to work on the problem. These experts in illusion formed a study group to build, test and photograph possible solutions.

In the fall of 1941, Ohmer was sent by the Army to Hawaii to assess its defenses. He returned with a plan to camouflage Wheeler Field on Oahu. The cost: $50,000. The Army declined.

On Dec 7th, 1941, the Imperial Japanese Air Force bombed Pearl Harbor. The United States was in the war. Douglas' camouflage went into full swing, and Ohmer and the Army Corps of Engineers came in to build it. Among Ohmer's greatest contributions to the war effort was his camouflage of large-scale industrial plants. The Santa Monica Douglas Factory was his first. (By 1942 he was in charge of disguising highways, facilities and 34 military airfields along the entire West coast from the Aleutians to California.)

Back at the Douglas Factory, 400 steel poles were erected (each 90 feet tall), on top of which 4 million square feet of wire mesh, held in tension-compression, created the structure for an elaborate illusion over a mile long. The factory was underneath, and spread above was a fake neighborhood, with fake houses, trees and streets. The camouflage was an unreal world of theatrical hard-wall flat houses only five feet tall, which was all that was needed to recreate the illusion of the factory as seen from the air.

Above: Fake streets and homes are added to the top of the Douglas factory. Notice the fake streets line up perfectly with real streets.

Below: Mesh camouflage covers production area storing aircraft parts.

Above: A worker walks between buildings underneath a mesh landscape of camouflage above.

Below: To create the illusion of cars on the street, Hollywood set designers molded sheet metal into a shape of a 1940 Ford. Notice the headlamps have different shapes.

Trees were made from chicken wire and cloth with painted feather leaves wired to them, and fake clotheslines held dangling laundry, hung out in the breeze at regular intervals. The factory's air ducts became street fire hydrants, while steam released from the factory floated up from fake chimneys perched on houses made of canvas.

Above: Local children walking to school past the camouflaged airport were sometimes alarmed by the sight of fake cows, "grazing" on the newly made hillsides. What became of the fake cows? After the war, they returned to the Warner Brothers prop department in Burbank to star in the Warner Brothers television westerns of the 1950's.

The runway and taxiways were painted to look like agriculture; the hangars, factory and parking lots were covered up. The camouflage sloped up from the level ground, looking like just another hill. When it rained, pieces of the camo and paint showered down on anything below.

Underneath, forty thousand people worked twenty-four hours a day in three shifts. The employees were mostly women. Everyone from the engineers and senior managers to the riveters, wiring and sheet metal workers, most were women, and women of color. This is not how it had been before the war, and unfortunately these opportunities did not last after the war.

There were dugout positions inside the factory, surrounded by sandbags. If the factory was bombed, you could dive for cover. There was an anti-aircraft gun battery at the railroad tracks where Bergamot Station is now, also guns at the west end of the runway, in Mar Vista on the hills below the south side of the runway, and at the softball diamond above Centinela on the east side of the runway.

Huge hot air balloons attached to long lines floated in the sky around the airport, making it an obstacle course to fly around the area. These "Barrage Balloons" were anchored by enormous concrete blocks sunk into the ground. The balloons themselves were mechanically released to fly higher at night, because an attacking airplane would fly higher at night. (All airplanes fly higher at night. If something goes wrong, you are higher above the ground and have more time to fix the problem.)

The camouflage was up for the duration of the war, and it served its intended purpose: Pilots flying over the area were unable to locate the airport by sight. The airport was not exactly invisible, just hard enough to find that if a pilot flying in off the ocean at 8,000 feet had just one pass to find the airport, fly over and bomb it, the pilot's confusion and momentary delay would arouse enough suspicion and allow enough time to shoot the invading airplane down. It didn't happen, but they were ready.

Above: This aerial view of the Santa Monica Airport shows how hidden the factory and runway were for enemy aircraft. If you look closely you will see a fake factory and runway on the left side of the photo.

Above: This diagram shows the location of the fake runway, factory and real runway, factory. The runway was so well hidden, that some pilots from other locations diverted their flight because they assumed the airport wasn't there.

Above: A woman poses for a picture lounging, in a small park in the fake community above the factory.

Below: A couple walk around inspecting their fake house. Note the house is only five feet tall—enough to fool pilots in the air and appear normal in aerial photographs.

Above: A C-47 sits just outside of the camouflageof the factory edge.

Below: Camouflage covers Douglas employee parking, making it look more like a field.

Above: Employees worked beneath the camouflage, rain or shine.

"Rosie the Riveter"

Rosie the Riveter isn't really one woman, she is millions of women. The name came from a popular song, then an illustration on the cover of the magazine the Saturday Evening Post.

After late 1941, the Department of Labor began a campaign to call on women to join the workforce and take up the industrial labor to replace the men who went to war. Sixteen million total men and women went off to war, and 8 million women stepped into the workforce. Minority workers such as African Americans and Latinos found employment opportunities such as never before.

Above: Aircraft Workers Lucille Little (left) and Amanda Smith (middle photo) working at the Douglas Aircraft Company in Long Beach, California.
Right: 1943, Marion Schultz, Douglas Aircraft Company, Santa Monica, CA.
(IMAGE: Library of Congress)

By 1943, more than 50% of the workforce were women working in factories all over the United States, building ships, airplanes, vehicles and other products necessary for the war effort. With the help of women workers, total industrial production doubled between 1939 and 1945. The military production was astounding: 300,000 aircraft, 12,000 ships, 86,000 tanks, and 64,000 landing craft in addition to millions of artillery pieces and small weapons.

Women worked in positions previously closed to them, yet the aviation industry saw the greatest increase in female workers. More than 310,000 women worked in the U.S. aircraft industry in 1943, representing 65 percent of the industry's total workforce (compared to just 1 percent in the pre-war years).

The symbol of Rosie was larger than just one riveter. She was the millions of women who answered the call.

The DC-3

Made at Santa Monica Airport, this plane changed the world

The DC-3 first flew on Dec 17th, 1935, taking off from Douglas' home field at the Santa Monica Airport 32 years to the day after the Wright Brother's first flight.

Commercial air travel in the early 1930s was tiring, very loud and difficult. Only the brave, those suffering an emergency or up against an implacable deadline flew long flights. Then, in1931, safety concerns added to the problems and became a public priority overnight. The crash of an all-wood Fokker F10, flown by Transcontinental and Western Air (TWA) killed eight people, one of whom was a beloved sports hero of the day, Knut Rockne, head football coach at the University of Notre Dame, and possibly the most winning football coach of all time. Crashes had happened before, but this one focused the public's and authorities' attention. Urgency was generated to better the industry.

Demands were made to improve aircraft design and construction, and airlines industry practices.

The wooden Fokker had gone down over Kansas in severe wind and icing conditions, and there were suggestions that the wood frame of the airplane had failed. The push was on to create all-metal aircraft, aluminum, hollow-shelled airplanes to provide a strong and

1927-31: Fokker F10 Trimotor Aircraft seats 12 passengers.

streamlined structure. Other safety upgrades were to follow: the development of supercharged engines increased power, new controllable-pitch propellers created more thrust for takeoff and improved performance overall. De-icing equipment was introduced.

These upgrades were the eventual result. Immediately after the accident, the airlines turned to the already available Ford Tri-motor airplanes. These slow, boxy, three engine airplanes were similar to the Fokker F10 which had crashed, except they were all metal. They were sturdy and spacious, but slow in the air and expensive to build.

Ford Tri Motor Airplane (Image: EAA)

Boeing developed their 247, a plane that introduced many safety features that would eventually become standard. But the parent

company of Boeing, at that time United Aircraft, also the parent
company of United Airlines, had
monopolized all the available
Boeing 247s and all the 247s yet
to be built.

So, TWA, in its urgency to upgrade
its airplanes and hold onto its
flying customers, turned to
Douglas Aircraft in Santa Monica.
The DC-1 and DC-2 were the result.

Boeing 247 Airplane. Circa 1933
(Image: Wikipedia)

The DC-2 (DC standing for Douglas Commercial as opposed to
Douglas' military planes) took advantage of the Boeing 247s
upgrades and went further. The DC-2 was faster, had greater
range and could carry more payload. The widening of its fuselage
to carry 21 passengers into what became the DC-3 made it the
first airplane to make airlines actually profitable. People began
flying in record numbers.

In 1934, just before the DC-3, a flight from New York to Los Angles
was a usually 25-hour long ordeal, involving at least two airlines,
two changes of planes and as many as 16 stops. Flying the
Boeing 247 and even the DC-2, passengers would usually fly
shorter legs during the day, and often take a train at night. With
the DC-3, a single airplane could cross the country in about 15
hours, usually stopping only three times to refuel.

The airlines became profitable. Douglas Aircraft became wildly
profitable and in extension, the workers of Santa Monica were
spared the long, grim economic depression of the 1930s. Workers
by the thousands flocked to Santa Monica to make the DC-3 and
the city escaped the unemployment and poverty that was the
reality of many during the time.

Douglas Aircraft did not consider the DC-3 a sensational phenomenon: it was simply the next logical development of the DC-1 and DC-2.

Above: In April 1936, the first Douglas Sleeper Transport was delivered to American Airlines. Douglas Engineer Arthur E. Raymond designed the DC-3 as a luxury airliner for American Airlines, flying either 21 seats or 14-berth sleeper services for overnight flights, complete with dressing rooms, a 'honeymoon cabin,' and a galley serving hot meals, from New York to Chicago.

The first DC-3 ever built was actually a modified version of the DC-2 for American Airlines. They ordered a longer version of the DC-2 plane and it became known as the Douglas Sleeper Transport. This was the first DC-3 ever built and it was the utmost in luxury. Fourteen plush seats in four main compartments could be folded to form seven berths, while seven more folded down from the cabin ceiling. The plane accommodated 14 overnight passengers or 28 for shorter daytime flights. The first plane was delivered to American Airlines in June 1936, followed two months later by the first standard 21-passenger DC-3. In November 1936, United Airlines became the second DC-3 customer. These first orders were soon followed by orders from more than 30 other airlines in the next two years. **By 1939, more than 90 percent of the nation's airline passengers were flying on DC-2s and DC-3s.**

In 1936 (only one year after its first flight) Royal Dutch Airlines, (KLM) was flying a DC-3 service from Amsterdam to Sydney, Australia.

The Romance of Travel

The DC-3 was also glamorous. It took hold of the imagination of people who had only ever dreamed of travelling. Service was something modern airline passengers now can only imagine. Once on board, "guests" were offered cocktails, followed by entrée choices such as steak or duckling, served on china with specially marked silverware. Transcontinental sleeper flights featured curtained berths with goose-down comforters and feather mattresses.

Above Left: 1933. Interior of Douglas DC-1 with passengers. Notice it seats about a dozen.
Above Right: DC-3 seating with almost 21 passengers, almost double the amount of a DC-1. (Image: California State College).

Instantly acclaimed as a very beautiful airplane, the photogenic DC-3 captured the spirit of travel. It was, and still is, lovely from every angle.

Above: A DC-3 flying over the Hudson in New York, NY. (Image: Life Magazine)

Douglas Engineer Arthur E. Raymond led the team who designed the DC-3. He later worked on the Gemini and Apollo space missions for NASA. Raymond also helped found the RAND Corp., the renowned Santa Monica-based think tank, which began in 1946 as an offshoot of the Douglas Aircraft Company. But Raymond was best known for his work with Douglas, specifically his work on the DC-3.

The stunning success of the DC-3 was due in part to its new engines, made by Wright then by Pratt & Whitney. The super-charged twin engines developed 1,200 horsepower each, so the DC-3 could carry 21 passengers at a cruising speed of 195 miles per hour, with a range of 1,380 miles. The faster speed made a coast to coast flight in 15 hours possible. Its speediest competitor could only deliver a 19-hour flight.

"The DC-3 was an airplane built in a time when product life was designed to be indefinite," Douglas Engineer Arthur Raymond remarked to the Los Angeles Times in 1985, on the DC-3's 50th anniversary.

The C-47

The military version of the DC-3

Dwight D. Eisenhower, First Supreme Allied Commander, Europe, during World War II and 34th President of the United States, stated that the DC-3 was one of the single pieces of equipment which did the most to win the war. (The others were the Jeep, the bulldozer, the two-and-a-half-ton truck and the six-wheel drive amphibious vehicle known as the DUKW, or the "duck".)

Before World War II, 413 DC-3s had been made for the airlines. During World War II, Douglas mass-produced the military variant of the DC-3, called the C-47, (C standing for Cargo.) Over 12,000 C-47 military transports and all their variants were made during World War II, most of them made at Santa Monica Airport.

The armed forces of many countries flew the C-47 for the transport of troops, cargo, and wounded. The U.S. Navy designation was R4D. About 2,000 C-47s (received under lend-lease) in British and Commonwealth service took the name "Dakota", inspired by the acronym "DACoTA" for Douglas Aircraft Company Transport Aircraft.

The C-47s were made in the Douglas factories in Santa Monica, Long Beach California and Oklahoma City, Oklahoma. As C-47s rolled off the line, their 1,500-horsepower radial engines shook the air day and night. Most C-47s were made in Santa Monica, where DC-3s had been made all along.

Easy to fly, (extremely pilot friendly), simple to maintain, and able to take off and land on short distances from dirt strips and grass runways, the DC-3 was a natural military transport plane when war broke out between the United States and Japan in 1941.

For both airline and military use, the DC-3 proved to be tough, flexible, and easy to operate and maintain. Its exploits during the war became the stuff of legend.

Above: Paratroopers jumped out of C-47s on D-Day. Wounded were medevac'd out of the islands in the South Pacific in it. It was instrumental in the Berlin Airlift. It was simply one of the most durable planes ever built. (Image: Keystone/Getty)

The C-47 was vital to the success of many Allied campaigns, in particular those at Guadalcanal and in the jungles of New Guinea and Burma, where the C-47 and its naval version, the R4D, made it possible for Allied troops to counter the mobility of the light-traveling Japanese army. Additionally, C-47s were used to airlift supplies to the embattled American forces during the Battle of Bastogne.

Possibly its most influential role in military aviation, however, was flying supplies "over the hump," better known as the Himalayas, from India into China. This expertise was later used in the Berlin Airlift, in which the C-47 played a major role, until the aircraft were replaced by Douglas C-54 Skymasters.

In Europe, the C-47 (and a specialized paratroop variant, the Douglas C-53 Skytrooper) was used in huge numbers in the later stages of the war, particularly to tow gliders and drop paratroops. Allied paratroop operations relied on the Dakota, as British called it. Thousands flew during the invasion of Sicily, D-Day, and Arnhem. During the invasion of Sicily in July 1943, C-47s dropped 4,381 Allied paratroops. More than 50,000 paratroops were dropped by C-47s during the first few days of the invasion of Normandy, France, in June 1944.

In the Pacific War, with careful use of the island landing strips of the Pacific Ocean, C-47s were even used for ferrying soldiers serving in the Pacific theater back to the United States.

Above: C-47s unloading at Tempelhof Airport during the Berlin Airlift. DC-3s were among the heroes of the Berlin Airlift of 1948-9 when Allied aircraft fed

Berlin as Stalin tried to starve the city into Soviet submission. If ever an aircraft deserved honors, it was the Douglas DC-3.

The DC-3 by all its names became so well-known and respected during World War II that after the war, military DC-3s became the mainstay of the newly formed and established airlines around the globe. Douglas stopped building the DC-3 in 1946, the last one produced was sold to Belgium's Sabena Airlines.

For years after the war, the C-47 was a key part of the military's air fleet, and saw duty in Korea. More than 30 years after its first flight the C-47 flew missions in Vietnam, where as a gunship it was known as "Spooky" and "Puff the Magic Dragon."

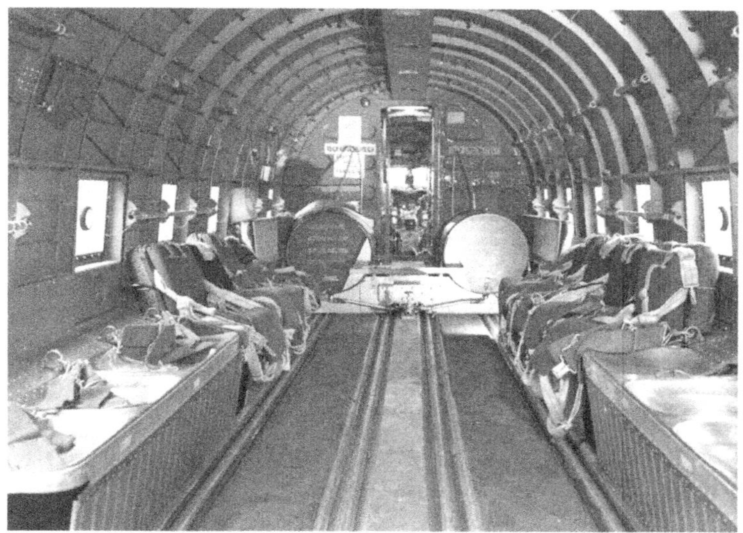

Above: Interior C-47 troop transport while empty (Image: Wikipedia)

Below: Interior of C-47 with ~17 paratroopers (Image: US Library of Congress)

Above: The C-47 would often transport troops into the battle field, and then be used as a medical evacuation tool on a return mission by ferring wounded troups back to safety. Although primitive, it was very effective. Image: US Army Air Forces

By war's end, 10,692 of the DC-3/C-47 aircraft had been built. From its pioneering of military airlifts over the Hump, to its perfecting of the technique during the Berlin Airlift, the C-47 has been prized for its versatility and dependability, factors that explain its remarkable longevity as an active carrier worldwide.

WWII C-47 Pilot Interview

The true story of a pilot who flew the C-47, one of the many planes made at Douglas Aircraft at Santa Monica Airport.

My name is Harry Albaugh. Most of my friends called me "Tex" because I was born in San Antonio, Texas. I attended Rice University in Houston. In 1939, the clouds of war were on the horizon, so I decided to put my college career on hold, and joined the Army Air Corps as a flying cadet.

My first assignment was to Sacramento Air Depot and then on to the China-India-Burma Theater (CBI) with the 10th Weather Squadron in New Delhi, India. I arrived in New Delhi in the summer of 1943.

Harry "Tex" Albaugh (second from right) during WWII standing in front of a Douglas C-47.

I flew the C-47 (the military version of the DC-3), 157 times over

the Himalaya Mountains between India and China during World War II. Flying this route was a dangerous thing to do, but our mission was an important one. We were carrying fuel and supplies to support allied efforts to defeat the Japanese in China. One-in-three of my fellow pilots who flew that route didn't make it home. I was very fortunate to have been able to safely fly it so many times.

We called the C-47 "Betsy" and I am pretty sure that many of the planes I flew were built at Santa Monica Airport. I have fond memories of the C-47. It was a great airplane to fly (and the right plane at the right time during the war effort to that allowed us to deliver supplies to those in need. Many people called it the "pickup truck in the sky").

Like all airplanes, old "Betsy" had limitations. The C-47 could only fly so high with a load of supplies. The air gets thinner at high altitudes and it was harder for Betsy's propellers to "bite" into the air and help us climb with so much weight onboard. Sometimes the mountains along our route were higher than we were able to fly (15,000 feet at times), so we would fly between mountain peaks when we had to.

Above: C47 flying the Hump (Image: R G Smith)

The wind and weather were always dangerous. Sometimes the downdrafts over the mountains would push our plane down faster than we could climb, even at full power. Some of my friends were pushed into the mountains by the weather and winds. Many of my fellow pilots did not survive the hump.

The Hump was the name given by Allied pilots in the Second World War to the eastern end of the Himalayan Mountains over which they flew military transport aircraft from India to China to resupply the Chinese war effort of Chiang Kai-shek and the units of the United States Army Air Forces based in China. The Hump was one of the deadliest cargo flights in history. It killed about 30% of all allied aircrews who attempted the flight (700 Allied planes crashed or got shot down and 1,200 airmen died).

DC-3 in the 1950s

In the 1950s, about 150 scheduled airlines in 70 countries were using 6,000 DC-3s. In commercial operations alone, by the 1950s, the DC-3 had flown more than 7 billion scheduled miles, 290,000 times around the world, not including military, private or executive use. American Airlines, in its 13 years of using the DC-3, noted that their 94 aircraft carried 10.5 million passengers for an almost unbelievable total of 4.6 billion passenger miles. These numbers do not include the extensive cargo and non-scheduled flight hours the DC-3s have flown since.

Today hundreds of DC-3s are still flying carrying passengers or cargo. The exact number is unknown, there are believed to be about 400 still flying. One based in Oregon has more than 91,000 hours on its durable airframe. One flies regularly scheduled flights from Long Beach Airport to Catalina Island. One DC-3 flies freight between the islands in Hawaii, others have been spotted in Siberia, Iceland, Canada, the Caribbean, France, parts of Africa, South America and Antarctica. They are used for passenger travel and cargo hauling, crop spraying and firefighting, rescue work, research and exploration, parachute training and for the joy of flying one of the best airplanes ever made, on its way to celebrating its one hundred years of flying.

The Aero Theatre

Few people know that this little Montana Avenue theater in Santa Monica has roots in aviation during the war years.

Above: The Aero Theatre, 1942. The State Guard poses in front of the Aero Theatre. "Kings Row" starring Ronald Reagan is playing at the theater along with an "Andy Hardy" film, a popular series of films starring Mickey Rooney. (Image: Emerson Gaze)

The tiny Aero Theatre, tucked into the neighborhood on Montana and 14th Street at the far north end of Santa Monica, is about as far as you can go from the airport and still be in Santa Monica. The Aero was built by Donald Douglas in 1939 as a real estate investment, along with five retail spaces nearby. (The name "Aero" gently references the theater's aviation roots). What started as land investment became a welcome benefit for the Douglas employees. By 1939, Santa Monica was an aircraft town and Douglas wanted his employees to have recreation with physical distance from their workplace. With the theater located up on Montana Avenue, the moviegoers could feel they had left work and were not in sight of the factory. Admission was 20 cents for adults, 10 cents for children, screening double features that changed three times a week. War production at the factory ran 24 hours a day so the Aero ran movies 24 hours a day. You got off work at 2 a.m.; you could still go to the 2:30 am showing of a movie.

The Supersonic 1950s

The D-558-I Skystreak 1947 to 1953. Made by Douglas Aircraft at the Santa Monica Airport. Less well known than the X-1, the D-558-I could carry out research roles that complemented those of the more glamorous, rocket-powered craft.

The D-558-I "Skystreak", made from 1947 to 1953, was among the early transonic research airplanes such as the X-1, X-4, X-5, and XF-92A. Only three single-seat, straight-wing D-558-I Skystreaks were ever made. They flew in a joint program involving the National Advisory Committee for Aeronautics (NACA), the Navy-Marine Corps, and the Douglas Aircraft Company.

The Skystreaks, built by Douglas Aircraft in Santa Monica, set two world speed records one of 640.744 miles per hour, then it broke its own record a week later and flew 650.606 miles an hour.

Transonic research airplanes were designed to meet two needs of the early 1940s. One was for accurate wind tunnel data for speeds in the range of roughly Mach 0.8 to 1.2. The other was that aircraft like the P-38 "Lightning" were approaching Mach speeds in dives and breaking apart from the effects of compressibility-increased density and disturbed airflow as the speed approached that of sound, creating shock waves. The government needed an airplane with enough structural strength to withstand compressibility in the transonic region. The AAF preferred a rocket-powered aircraft and funded the X-1. The NACA and Navy preferred a more conservative design and pursued the D-558 Skystreak (a mixed rocket/jet-powered configuration).

The Navy contracted with Douglas to design the Skystreak. Headed by Edward H. Heinemann, the Douglas design team, used NACA information and airfoil shapes and tested its models in NACA and California Institute of Technology wind tunnels. It relied on NACA recommendations, such as putting the horizontal stabilizer high on the vertical tail to avoid the wake from the wing.

The fuselage used magnesium alloys extensively, while the wings were fabricated from more conventional at the time aluminum alloys. The airframe was designed to withstand unusually high loads of up to 18 times gravity due to the uncertainties of transonic flight.

Douglas pilot Eugene F. May flew the number one Skystreak for the first time on April 14, 1947. This test flight obtained data about flight in that speed range not yet available from tests in existing wind tunnels.

When Commander Turner F. Caldwell set the world's speed record in the D-558-I. Overall, the three Skystreaks, equipped with Allison J-35-A-11 turbojet engines, gathered a great deal of data on handling qualities. This data was then available for the designers of new military aircraft.

The Skystreak lacked an ejection seat. The design team had considered one, but given the available technology the team discovered that the force necessary to propel the seat and pilot higher than the vertical tail exceeded the pilot's physiological limits. Therefore, Douglas provided instead a jettisonable nose capsule from which the pilot could bail out if the airplane were high enough.

The Douglas "Skyrocket"

The large B29 (on top) launches the smaller, sleeker and faster Skyrocket (1948-1956). The Skyrocket was made by Douglas Aircraft at the Santa Monica Airport.

The D-558-II "Skyrocket", 1948-1956, was built by Douglas for the NACA and the Navy. The mission of the D-558-II program was to investigate the flight characteristics of a swept-wing aircraft at high supersonic speeds.

The Skyrocket was a single-place, 35-degree swept-wing aircraft measuring 42 feet in length. It was 12 feet, 8 inches in height and had a wingspan of 25 feet. Fully fueled it weighed from about 10,572 lbs to 15,787 lbs depending on configuration. Only three were made. The first of the three D-558-IIs had a Westinghouse J34-40 jet engine and took off under its own power. The second was equipped with a turbojet engine replaced in 1950 with a Reaction Motors Inc. LR8-RM-6 rocket engine. This aircraft was modified so it could be air-launched from a P2B-1S (Navy designation for the B-29) carrier aircraft. The third Skyrocket had the jet engine and the rocket engine but was also modified so it could be air-launched. The jet engine was for takeoff and climbing to altitude and the four-chambered rocket engine was for reaching supersonic speeds. The rocket engine was rated at 6,000 pounds of thrust. The D-558-II was first flown on Feb. 4, 1948, by John Martin, a Douglas test pilot. An NACA pilot, Scott Crossfield, became the first person to fly faster than twice the speed of sound when he piloted the D-558-II to its maximum speed of Mach 2.005 (1,291 mph) at 62,000 feet altitude on Nov. 20, 1953. Its peak altitude, 83,235 feet, a record in its day, was reached with Lt. Col. Marion Carl at the controls.

A swept wing is a wing which angles either backward or, occasionally, forward, from its root rather than in a straight sideways direction. Wing sweep has the effect of delaying the shock waves and accompanying aerodynamic drag rise caused by fluid compressibility near the speed of sound, improving performance.

The X-3 Stiletto

The X-3 Stiletto, a jet-powered research aircraft manufactured by the Douglas Aircraft Company at Santa Monica Airport from 1953-1955. IMAGE: NASA

The primary mission of the X-3 Stiletto was to investigate the design features of an aircraft for suitable sustained supersonic speeds.

Douglas Aircraft at Santa Monica built the only model of the X-3 ever produced. It was 66 feet, 9 inches long; 12 feet, 6 inches high; and had a wingspan of 22 feet, 8 inches. Two Westinghouse J34 turbojets, equipped with afterburners, powered the X-3. It was capable of takeoff and landing under its own power.

The top speed of the aircraft was 700 miles per hour, just under the speed of sound. A secondary purpose of the X-3 was to test new materials such as titanium, and it also contributed to the development of aircraft tire technology.

Bill Lear

In 1949, Bill Lear opened a manufacturing facility on a ten-acre parcel on the south side of the Santa Monica Airport on Bundy. The company grew to 5,000 employees.

 "There are two kinds of inventors. The inventor who just likes to be clever and come up with a new idea. And the inventor who realizes there's a need and tries to fill it. I have spent my whole life discovering needs and then finding ways to fulfill them." – Bill Lear, 1972.

Bill Lear, whose company was headquartered at Santa Monica Airport from 1965 on, had only an eighth-grade education. Lear held more than 150 patents and is credited with inventing the car radio, the eight-track stereo tape player and cartridges, the autopilot for jet aircraft, the navigational radio, and the radio direction-finder for general aviation aircraft.

When Bill Lear was 17 in 1919, he found a job as a mechanic at an airport in Chicago, repairing some of the first air-mail planes. He took his paycheck in the form of flying lessons.

Fascinated with radio technology, he went into business for himself. He formed his own companies, including the Lear Radio Laboratory in Tulsa (1924 to 1928), and was part owner of Galvin Manufacturing Company (1926 to 1930) in Chicago. At Galvin, which became the Motorola Corp., Lear developed the first car radio, which Motorola mass-produced with great success. In 1930, Lear took his profits and founded a few more companies under his name. Before his companies created jets, they developed aerospace instruments and electronics. In 1935, Lear invented the

Lear-O-Scope, one of the first commercial radio compasses and the Learmatic Navigator in 1940.

In 1950, President Harry Truman gave Lear the Collier Trophy for the F-5 autopilot, the first ever for jets.

By 1962, Lear's company, now headquartered at the Santa Monica Airport, had 5,000 employees. Plants were located in California, also Germany, Michigan and Ohio. Bill Lear sold his interest in company located in Santa Monica. This sale financed his company that created the iconic jets that carry his name.

Above: The prototype for the Learstar N4848V at the Lear factory at Santa Monica. An early Lear Hangar still stands at Santa Monica Airport.

Below: A modern day image of the headquarters of Lear Astronics, the 4 story building built by Bill Lear now houses the Bundy Campus of the Santa Monica City College.

Made in Santa Monica: The Big 1950's

In the post war 1940s and into the 1950s, aircraft manufacturers, including Douglas Aircraft, introduced new, large, four engine airliners. These larger airliners developed after World War II, were designed with an eye on the new, profitable, transcontinental air routes. The new aircraft allowed the airlines to carry many more people farther, at faster speeds, with greater comfort and made money for the airlines at a record rate. There was a boom. Competition increased, fares fell and more markets opened up to air travel than ever before.

The DC-4

The four-engine DC-4 improved safety and comfort for the flying public. The still unpressurized DC-4 could carry 44 passengers. Both the DC-4 and the military version, the C-54, were a popular and reliable airplane. 1,245 were built between 1942 and 1947. Western Airlines started flying the 4 in January of 1946, and United began flying them coast-to-coast three months later. The DC-4 flight United's "Mainliner 230," flew New York to San Francisco in 16 hours with a stop at Chicago. The DC-4 was expensive to maintain, but the $236.60 round trip ticket was 26 percent cheaper than prewar fares.

The DC-5

The DC-5 is the least known and least produced of the famous DC airliners. It was a 16 to 22 passenger, twin-engine propeller plane designed for shorter routes than the DC-3 or DC-4. By the time it was ready in 1940, airlines were canceling orders. Consequently, only five civilian DC-5s were built. Douglas Aircraft was already switching over to military production of the C-47, the DC-5 was taken over by the war production. Twelve military variants were produced as the RD3D-2. It is interesting to note that the prototype DC-5 was bought by William Boeing to be his personal airplane, modified to seat 16 passengers. Many years later the Douglas Aircraft Company would be bought by Boeing.

The DC-6

Image: Jon Proctor

Douglas Aircraft's response to the classic Lockheed Constellation, the 6 was slightly longer than the DC-4 and competitively pressurized like the "Connie". The DC-6 carried 60 passengers and had heating components in its wings to prevent icing. United introduced the DC-6 in 1947. After initial problems were overcome, the DC-6 became a widely flown airliner.

The DC-6B

Above: The Douglas DC-6B flying in 2011 (Image: MyPics.at)

The 6B was perhaps the most successful piston-engine airline design ever made. It was known for its reliability, efficiency of operation and sheer toughness. Its slightly stretched fuselage allow it to carry 88 passengers. United bought them in 1952 and Pan Am was able to use them to introduce new "tourist fares" on flights across the Atlantic.

The DC-7

Above: The military version of the Douglas DC-7 (the C-121A), flew non-tactical missions in the 1950s, under the command of the Military Air Transport Service. (Image: AirportJournals.com)

American introduced the 7 on its New York to LA flights in November of 1953. The DC-7 cruised at 350 miles per hour and was the first airliner to be able to complete nonstop transcontinental service in both directions across the country. Three hundred and thirty-eight DC-7s were bought by 18 different airlines. It carried 60 passengers between the two coasts in under 8 hours. The fare was $159 one way and $302 round trip.

The DC-7C

Douglas expanded its propeller-driven commercial airliner business with the production of the 166,000-pound DC-7C. The 7C or "7 Seas" as it was called, flew 110 passengers at up to 400 mph for in excess of 5,600 miles. Douglas stretched the fuselage of the DC-7 forty-two inches and lengthening the wings by inserting a five-foot extension at each wing root. This gave the new DC-7C "Seven Seas" more room for fuel, and also positioned the engines further out on the wing, decreasing the engine noise and vibration to the passengers. More powerful 3400 hp engines were added. These improvements grew the range on the 7C to 5635 miles, allowing non-stop routes never before possible with Douglas aircraft. The "Seven Seas" service was introduced by Pan Am in June 1956, and 121 7C's were eventually made, the most of the DC aircraft series. The DC-7C went on to fly non-stop routes across the US, as well as in transatlantic, transpacific, and even Great Circle routes over the North Pole.

The DC-7C was the last production aircraft built in Santa Monica.

Above: The DC-3, DC-4, DC-6 and DC-7 all lined up at Santa Monica Airport in 1953 looking east. The street on the right is National Blvd.

In 1959, Douglas developed the DC-8 jet to compete with Boeing's 707, and proposed that the City of Santa Monica lengthen the runway to accommodate this new aircraft. The City declined. Douglas moved its jet manufacturing to the Long Beach Airport, dramatically growing the fortunes of the Long Beach area.

Research and development, missile production, NASA projects and sub-assembly work continued at the Santa Monica Airport plant for some time, but the big airplanes and the jobs making them moved south.

The accomplishments of Douglas Aircraft are many.

Some of them include pioneering advances in areas related to aviation: ejection seats, air-to-air missiles, surface-to-air missiles, and air-to-surface missiles, launch rockets, bombs, and bomb racks. For NASA, Douglas built the Saturn SI-VB launch vehicle used for early orbital tests of Apollo capsules and the Delta three stage boosters.

After 50 years at the Santa Monica Airport, Douglas closed down its Santa Monica factory, having manufactured over 10,000 aircraft at the SMO plant. Douglas started a local industry that became an economic powerhouse that forever changed the way the world flies.

The Importance of SMO

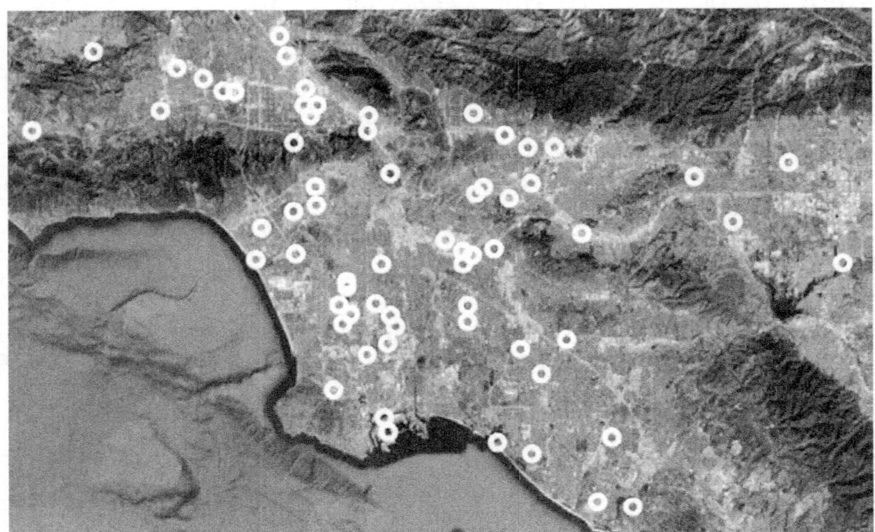

Above: In the early days, there were 66 general-aviation airports in Los Angeles (locations marked by white circles on the map), allowing people to avoid rough and rocky dirt roads, or no roads at all, and fly almost anywhere they wanted.

The Santa Monica airport today is a vibrant place, filled with activity and places to explore. The airport invites you to discover what it has to offer and change your perspective. There are over 100 businesses here, and 1,500 people make their living here. There are aviation businesses, flight schools, art galleries, restaurants and wonderful places to watch aircraft and meet new friends.

In the beginning, there were as many as 66 general-aviation airports in the greater Los Angeles area. Now, there are only nine.

Once an airport is closed, it can never be brought back to life. The land is usually repurposed into high-density buildings and complexes, condos, and retail. This can be good for developers, but repurposing the land in this way can take value from away from the community in many other ways.

The Santa Monica Airport is a resource. It is YOUR resource. An airport is like a bridge or freeway. You might not need it every day, but when you do, you want it to be there for safety and convenience. Airports, like roads, offer the opportunity to go somewhere new. They are a part of a network. Each piece of the network is a resource and makes the whole network more powerful. And in case of a crisis, the transportation network matters more than ever. The Santa Monica airport is a critical piece of emergency infrastructure, capable of handling the air operations necessary to get food, water and medicine to people in the area in case of a disaster.

Open Space Is Created by Santa Monica Airport

The Santa Monica Airport is a gem of open space and open air space in a congested city. Do you know why there are no tall buildings around the airport? No high rise business buildings on Ocean Park Boulevard? It isn't because builders decided they like low density-low rise buildings. It is because zoning laws protects the air space from being built up around the airport, on all sides of the airport. From south of Century City to the beach in Venice and Santa Monica areas, these areas would have no limits on height, and would have been already built up like Miami Beach or Honolulu, and without the airport they still could be. Your open view of the sky and limits on density are because of the airport, and are worth protecting.

Santa Monica Airport also operates as a protective bubble, keeping LAX traffic above 5,000 feet (and out of the air space of the smaller planes at SMO). Without SMO there, larger planes would be allowed to lower their flight path to as low as 3,500 feet (as many as 500 times per day). LAX has no curfew, so these planes can come in at any time (and they often do, even at 3 a.m.). These larger planes are extremely loud, and without SMO, the noise would affect all of Los Angeles. It's amazing how a "small" airport can have such a big impact on L.A.

Perhaps it is simply the intangibles, the airport is lovely. It is a place of industry, but maybe with its beautiful view of the mountains and shimmering view of sea at the end of the runway, it is more than a strip of concrete, it is part of the landscape of the imagination, the infrastructure of the spirit.

For all the brave and enterprising pilots and aircraft makers who flew and worked here (and still do), to the visitors from all over the world who come to see the famous airport, and of course to all the Junior Aviators: Thank you for coming to the Santa Monica Airport. We hope to see you again very soon!

Bibliography and Special Thanks

Thank you to the following people and resources that helped us to research information for this book:

Linda-Marie Koerner, Historian
Marissa Maynard
USC Library
UCLA Library
Santa Monica Library
SMGov.net
Time Magazine
Smithsonian.com
FlyingMag.com
Kern County Newspaper
CloverField.org
SMAA
Jim Ross
Boeing Images
LA Times
BBC.com
SeattleWorldCruiser.org
Wired.com
AirVectors.net
The Lockheed File
Adastron.com
DMairField.com

CentenialOfFlight.net
SantaMonicaMirror.com
CleavlandAirShow.com
Aerlex.com
ForgottenNewsmakers.com
VintageAirPhotos.blogspot.com
NationalWW2Museum.org
Wikipedia.org
Westland.net
EdCoatesCollection.com
MyPics.at
OneSixRight.com
Ots.ca.gov
Andre Bennett
Jim Ross
Bob Trimborn
Tony Bill
Joseph Miller
Melissa Dammer
Santa Monica Flyers
RGSmithArt.com

Journal Area

Include @SantaMonicaAir on social

Journal Area

Journal Area

Include @SantaMonicaAir on social

Journal Area

Journal Area

Include @SantaMonicaAir on social

Journal Area

Journal Area

Include @SantaMonicaAir on social

Journal Area

Printed in Dunstable, United Kingdom